Assessment Guide

Module E

HOLT McDOUGAL

HOUGHTON MIFFLIN HARCOURT

Acknowledgements for Covers

Cover Photo Credits

Volcanic eruption (bg) ©Photo Researchers, Inc.; *viscous lava* (l) ©Bruce Omori/epa/Corbis;
Mars Rover (cl) ©Mark Garlick/Photo Researchers, Inc.; *mushroom rock* (cr) ©John Elk III/Alamy;
anemometer (r) ©Ryan McGinnis/Flickr/Getty Images

Printed in the U.S.A.

ISBN 978-0-547-59317-3

4 5 6 7 8 9 10   0868   20 19 18 17 16 15 14 13 12
4500380852   A B C D E F G

Contents

INTRODUCTION

ASSESSMENT TOOLS

Unit 1 Earth's Surface

Unit 2 Earth's History

Unit 3 Minerals and Rocks

Unit 4 The Restless Earth

INTRODUCTION
Overview

ScienceFusion provides parallel instructional paths for teaching important science content. You may choose to use the print path, the digital path, or a combination of the two. The quizzes, tests, and other resources in this Assessment Guide may be used with either path.

The *ScienceFusion* assessment options are intended to give you maximum flexibility in assessing what your students know and what they can do. The program's formative and summative assessment categories reflect the understanding that assessment is a learning opportunity for students, and that students must periodically demonstrate mastery of content in cumulative tests.

All *ScienceFusion* tests are available—and editable—in ExamView and online at thinkcentral.com. You can customize a quiz or test for your classroom in many ways:

- adding or deleting items
- adjusting for cognitive complexity, Bloom's taxonomy level, or other measures of difficulty
- changing the sequence of items
- changing the item formats
- editing the question itself

All of these changes, except the last, can be made without invalidating the content correlation of the item.

This Assessment Guide is your directory to assessment in *ScienceFusion*. In it you'll find copymasters for Lesson Quizzes, Unit Tests, Unit Reviews, Performance-Based Assessments Alternative Assessments, and End-of-Module Tests; answers and explanations of answers; rubrics; a bubble-style answer sheet; and suggestions for assessing student progress using performance, portfolio, and other forms of integrated assessment.

You will also find additional assessment prompts and ideas throughout the program, as indicated on the chart that follows.

Assessment in *ScienceFusion* Program

	Student Editions	Teacher Edition	Assessment Guide	Digital Lessons	Online Resources at thinkcental.com	ExamView Test Generator
Formative Assessment						
Assessing Prior Knowledge						
Engage Your Brain	X					
Unit Pretest			X		X	X
Embedded Assessment						
Active Reading Questions	X					
Interactivities	X					
Probing Questions		X				
Formative Assessment		X				
Classroom Discussions		X				
Common Misconceptions		X				
Learning Alerts		X				
Embedded Questions and Tasks				X		
Student Self-Assessments				X		
Digital Lesson Quiz				X		
When used primarily for teaching						
Lesson Review	X	X				
Lesson Quiz			X		X	X
Alternative Assessment			X		X	
Performance-Based Assessment			X			
Portfolio Assessment, guidelines			X			
Summative Assessment						
End of Lessons						
Visual Summary	X	X				
Lesson Quiz			X		X	X
Alternative Assessment		X	X		X	
Rubrics			X		X	
End of Units						
Unit Review	X		X		X	X
Answers		X	X		X	
Test Doctor Answer Explanations		X	X			X
Unit Test A (on level)			X		X	X
Unit Test B (below level)			X		X	X
End of Module						
End-of-Module Test			X		X	X

Formative Assessment
Assessing Prior Knowledge

Frequently in this program, you'll find suggestions for assessing what your students already know before they begin studying a new lesson. These activities help you warm up the class, focus minds, and activate students' prior knowledge.

In This Assessment Guide

Each of the units begins with a Unit Pretest consisting of multiple-choice questions that assess prior and prerequisite knowledge. Use the Pretest to get a snapshot of the class and help you organize your pre-teaching.

In the Student Edition

Engage Your Brain Simple, interactive warm-up tasks get students thinking, and remind them of what they may already know about the lesson topics.

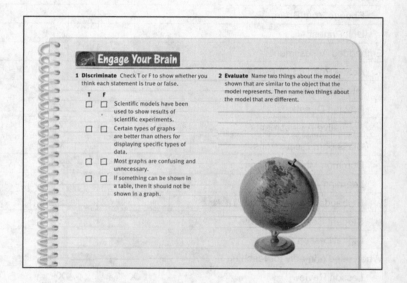

Active Reading Questions Students first see the lesson vocabulary on the opening page, where they are challenged to show what they know about the terms. Multiple exposures to the key terms throughout the lesson lead to mastery.

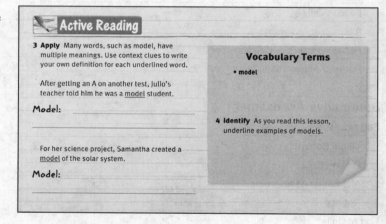

In the Teacher Edition

Opening Your Lesson At the start of each TE lesson Opening Your Lesson suggests questions and activities that help you assess prerequisite and prior knowledge.

Embedded Assessment

Once you're into the lesson, you'll continue to find suggestions, prompts, and resources for ongoing assessment.

Student Edition

Active Reading Questions and Interactivities Frequent questions and interactive prompts are embedded in the text, where they give students instant feedback on their comprehension. They ask students to respond in different ways, such as writing, drawing, and annotating the text. The variety of skills and response types helps all students succeed, and keeps them interested.

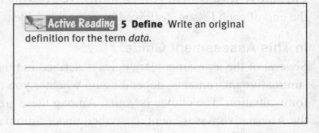

In the Teacher Edition

Probing Questions Probing questions appear in the point-of-use teaching suggestions. These questions are labeled to show the degree of independent inquiry they require. The three levels of inquiry—Directed, Guided, and Independent—give students experience that builds toward independent analysis.

Classroom Discussions Discussion is a natural opportunity to gauge how well students have absorbed the material, and to assess any misconceptions or gaps in their understanding. Students also learn from each other in this informal exchange. Classroom discussion ideas appear throughout the lesson in the Teacher Edition.

Tips for Classroom Discussions

- Allow students plenty of time to reflect and formulate their answers.

- Call upon students you sense have something to add but who haven't spoken.

- At the same time, allow reluctant students not to speak unless they choose to.

- Encourage students to respond to each other as well as to you.

Introduction
© Houghton Mifflin Harcourt Publishing Company

ix

Module E • Assessment Guide

Misconceptions and Learning Alerts The Teacher Background pages at the start of a unit describe common misconceptions and identify the lessons in which the misconceptions can be addressed. Strategies for addressing the misconceptions appear in the point-of-use teaching notes. Additional Learning Alerts help you introduce and assess challenging topics.

Formative Assessment A final formative assessment strategy appears on the Evaluate page at the end of each lesson, followed by reteaching ideas.

In This Assessment Guide

Several of the assessment strategies described in this book can be used either as formative or as summative instruments, depending on whether you use them primarily for teaching or primarily for evaluation. The choice is yours. Among these are the Lesson Quizzes, described here, and the Alternative Assessment, described under Summative Assessment, next. Because both of these assessments are provided for every lesson, you could use them both at different times.

Lesson Quizzes as Formative Assessment In this book, Lesson Quizzes in a unit follow the Unit Pretest. The five-item Lesson Quiz can be administered as a written test, used as an oral quiz, or given to small student groups for collaboration. In the Answer Key at the end of this book, you'll find a feature called the Test Doctor, which provides a brief explanation of what makes each correct answer correct and each incorrect answer incorrect. Use this explanatory material to begin a discussion following the quiz.

Classroom Observation

Classroom observation is one way to gather and record information that can lead to improved instruction. You'll find a Classroom Observation Checklist in Assessment Tools, following the Introduction.

Tips for Classroom Observation

- Don't try to see and record everything at once. Instead, identify specific skills you will observe in a session.

- Don't try to observe everyone at once. Focus on a few students at a time.

- Repeat observations at different times in order to identify patterns. This practice helps you validate or correct your impressions from a single time.

- Use the checklist as is or modify it to suit your students and your instruction. Fill in student names across the top and write the date next to the skills you are observing on a particular day.

- Keep the checklist, add to it, and consult it periodically for hints about strengths, weaknesses, and developments of particular students and of the class.

- Use your own system of ratings or the simple number code on the checklist. When you have not seen enough to give a rating, leave the space blank.

Summative Assessment

In the Student Edition

Visual Summary and Lesson Review

Interactive summaries help students synthesize lesson material, and the Lesson Review provides a variety of questions focusing on vocabulary, key concepts, and critical thinking.

Unit Reviews

Each unit in the Student Edition is followed by a Unit Review, also available in this Assessment Guide. These tests include the item types commonly found on the statewide assessments. You may want to use these tests to review unit content right away or at any time later in the year to help students prepare for the statewide assessment. If you wish to give students practice in filling in a machine-scorable answer sheet, use the bubble-type answer sheet at the start of the Answer Key.

In This Assessment Guide

Alternative Assessments

Every lesson has an Alternative Assessment worksheet, which is previewed in the Teacher Edition on the Evaluate page of the lesson. The activities on these worksheets assess student comprehension of core content, while at the same time offering a variety of options for students with various abilities, learning styles, and interests. The activities require students to produce a tangible product or to give a presentation that demonstrates their understanding of skills and concepts.

Tips for Alternative Assessment

- The structure of these worksheets allows for differentiation in topic, difficulty level, and activity type/learner preferences.

- Each worksheet has a variety of items for students and teachers to choose from.

- The items may relate to the entire lesson content or to just one or two key topics. Encourage students to select items so that they will hit most key topics in a lesson.

- Share the rubrics and Presentation Guidelines with students so they understand the expectations for these assignments. You could have them fill in a rubric with their name and activity choices at the same time they choose their assignments, and then submit the rubric with their presentation or assignment.

Grading Alternative Assessments

Each type of Alternative Assessment worksheet has a rubric for easy grading.

- The rubrics focus mostly on content comprehension, but also take into account presentation.

- The Answer Key describes the expected content mastery for each Alternative Assessment.

- Separate Presentation Guidelines describe the attributes of successful written work, posters and displays, oral presentations, and multimedia presentations.

- Each rubric has space to record your reasons for deducting points, such as content errors or particular presentation flaws.

- If you wish to change the focus of an Alternative Assessment worksheet, you can adjust the point values for the rubric.

The Presentation Guidelines and the rubrics follow the Introduction. The Answer Key appears at the end of the book.

Unit Tests A and B

This Assessment Guide contains leveled tests for each unit.

- The A-level tests are for students who typically perform below grade level.

- The B-level tests are intended for students whose performance is on grade level.

Both versions of the test address the unit content with a mixture of item types, including multiple choice, short response, and extended response. Both levels contains items of low, medium, and high cognitive complexity, though level B contains more items of higher complexity. A few items appear in both of the tests as a means of assuring parallel content coverage. If you need a higher-level test, you can easily assemble one from the lesson assessment banks in ExamView or online at thinkcentral.com. All items in the banks are tagged with five different measures of difficulty as well as standards and key terms.

End-of-Module Test

The final test in this Assessment Guide is the End-of-Module Review. This is a long-form, multiple-choice test in the style of the statewide assessments. An Answer Sheet appears with the review.

Performance-Based Assessment

Performance-Based Assessment involves a hands-on activity in which students demonstrate their skills and thought processes. Each Performance-Based Assessment includes a page of teacher-focused information and a general rubric for scoring. In addition to the Performance-Based Assessment provided for each unit, you can use many of the labs in the program as the basis for performance assessment.

Tips for Performance Assessment

- Prepare materials and stations so that all students have the same tasks. You may want to administer performance assessments to different groups over time.

- Provide clear expectations, including the measures on which students will be evaluated. You may invite them to help you formulate or modify the rubric.

- Assist students as needed, but avoid supplying answers to those who can handle the work on their own.

- Don't be hurried. Allow students enough time to do their best work.

Developing or Modifying a Rubric

Developing a rubric for a performance task involves three basic steps:

1. Identify the inquiry skills that are taught in the lesson and that students must perform to complete the task successfully and identify the understanding of content that is also required. Many of the skills may be found in the Lab and Activity Evaluation later in this guide.

2. Determine which skills and understandings of content are involved in each step.

3. Decide what you will look for to confirm that the student has acquired each skill and understanding you identified.

Portfolio Assessment, Guidelines

A portfolio is a showcase for student work, a place where many types of assignments, projects, reports and data sheets can be collected. The work samples in the collection provide snapshots of the student's efforts over time, and taken together they reveal the student's growth, attitudes, and understanding better than other types of assessment. Portfolio assessment involves meeting with each student to discuss the work and to set goals for future performance. In contrast with formal assessments, portfolio assessments have these advantages:

1. They give students a voice in the assessment process.
2. They foster reflection, self-monitoring, and self-evaluation.
3. They provide a comprehensive picture of a student's progress.

Tips for Portfolio Assessment

- Make a basic plan. Decide how many work samples will be included in the portfolios and what period of time they represent.

- Explain the portfolio and its use. Describe the portfolio an artist might put together, showing his or her best or most representative work, as part of an application for school or a job. The student's portfolio is based on this model.

- Together with your class decide on the required work samples that everyone's portfolio will contain.

- Explain that the students will choose additional samples of their work to include. Have students remember how their skills and understanding have grown over the period covered by the portfolio, and review their work with this in mind. The best pieces to choose may not be the longest or neatest.

- Give students the Portfolio Planning Worksheet found in Assessment Tools. Have students record their reasoning as they make their selections and assemble their portfolios.

- Share with students the Portfolio Evaluation Checklist, also found in Assessment Tools, and explain how you will evaluate the contents of their portfolios.

- Use the portfolios for conferences, grading, and planning. Give students the option of taking their portfolios home to share.

ASSESSMENT TOOLS
Alternative Assessment Presentation Guidelines

The following guidelines can be used as a starting point for evaluating student presentation of alternative assessments. For each category, use only the criteria that are relevant for the particular format you are evaluating; some criteria will not apply for certain formats.

Written Work
- Matches the assignment in format (essay, journal entry, newspaper report, etc.)
- Begins with a clear statement of the topic and purpose
- Provides information that is essential to the reader's understanding
- Supporting details are precise, related to the topic, and effective
- Follows a logical pattern of organization
- Uses transitions between ideas
- When appropriate, uses diagrams or other visuals
- Correct spelling, capitalization, and punctuation
- Correct grammar and usage
- Varied sentence structures
- Neat and legible

Posters and Displays
- Matches the assignment in format (brochure, poster, storyboard, etc.)
- Topic is well researched and quality information is presented
- Poster communicates an obvious, overall message
- Posters have large titles and the message, or purpose, is obvious
- Images are big, clear, and convey important information
- More important ideas and items are given more space and presented with larger images or text
- Colors are used for a purpose, such as to link words and images
- Sequence of presentation is easy to follow because of visual cues, such as arrows, letters, or numbers
- Artistic elements are appropriate and add to the overall presentation
- Text is neat
- Captions and labels have correct spelling, capitalization, and punctuation

Oral Presentations
- Matches the assignment in format (speech, news report, etc.)
- Presentation is delivered well, and enthusiasm is shown for topic
- Words are clearly pronounced and can easily be heard
- Information is presented in a logical, interesting sequence that the audience can follow
- Visual aids are relative to content, very neat, and artistic
- Often makes eye contact with audience
- Listens carefully to questions from the audience and responds accurately
- Stands straight, facing the audience
- Uses movements appropriate to the presentation; does not fidget
- Covers the topic well in the time allowed
- Gives enough information to clarify the topic, but does not include irrelevant details

Multimedia Presentations
- Topic is well researched, and essential information is presented
- The product shows evidence of an original and inventive approach
- The presentation conveys an obvious, overall message
- Contains all the required media elements, such as text, graphics, sounds, videos, and animations
- Fonts and formatting are used appropriately to emphasize words; color is used appropriately to enhance the fonts
- Sequence of presentation is logical and/or the navigation is easy and understandable
- Artistic elements are appropriate and add to the overall presentation
- The combination of multimedia elements with words and ideas produces an effective presentation
- Written elements have correct spelling, capitalization, and punctuation

Alternative Assessment Rubric – Tic-Tac-Toe

Worksheet Title: _____

Student Name: _____

Date: _____

Add the titles of each activity chosen to the chart below.

	Content *(0-3 points)*	**Presentation** *(0-2 points)*	*Points Sum*
Choice 1: _____			
Points			
Reason for missing points			
Choice 2: _____			
Points			
Reason for missing points			
Choice 3: _____			
Points			
Reason for missing points			
		Total Points (of 15 maximum)	

Alternative Assessment Rubric – Mix and Match

Worksheet Title: _____

Student Name: _____

Date: _____

Add the column choices to the chart below.

	Content (0-3 points)	Presentation (0-2 points)	Points Sum
Information Source from Column A: _____ Topics Chosen for Column B: _____ _____ Presentation Format from Column C: _____			
Points			
Reason for missing points			
		Total Points (of 5 maximum)	

Alternative Assessment Rubric – Take Your Pick

Worksheet Title: _____

Student Name: _____

Date: _____

Add the titles of each activity chosen to the chart below.

2-point item: 5-point item 8-point item:	**Content** *(0-1.5 points)* *(0-4 points)* *(0-6 points)*	**Presentation** *(0-0.5 point)* *(0-1 point)* *(0-2 points)*	***Points Sum***
Choice 1: _____			
Points			
Reason for missing points			
Choice 2: _____			
Points			
Reason for missing points			
		Total Points (of 10 maximum)	

Alternative Assessment Rubric – Choose Your Meal

Worksheet Title: _____

Student Name: _____

Date: _____

Add the titles of each activity chosen to the chart below.

Appetizer, side dish, or dessert: Main Dish	**Content** *(0-3 points)* *(0-6 points)*	**Presentation** *(0-2) points* *(0-4 points)*	***Points Sum***
Appetizer: _____			
Points			
Reason for missing points			
Side Dish: _____			
Points			
Reason for missing points			
Main Dish: _____			
Points			
Reason for missing points			
Dessert: _____			
Points			
Reason for missing points			
		Total Points (of 25 maximum)	

Alternative Assessment Rubric – Points of View

Worksheet Title: _____

Student Name: _____

Date: _____

Add the titles of group's assignment to the chart below.

	Content *(0-4 points)*	**Presentation** *(0-1 points)*	*Points Sum*
Point of View:			
Points			
Reason for missing points			
		Total Points (of 5 maximum)	

Alternative Assessment Rubric – Climb the Pyramid

Worksheet Title: _____

Student Name: _____

Date: _____

Add the titles of each activity chosen to the chart below.

	Content *(0-3 points)*	**Presentation** *(0-2 points)*	*Points Sum*
Choice from bottom row: _____			
Points			
Reason for missing points			
Choice from middle row: _____			
Points			
Reason for missing points			
Top row: _____			
Points			
Reason for missing points			
		Total Points (of 15 maximum)	

Alternative Assessment Rubric – Climb the Ladder

Worksheet Title: _____

Student Name: _____

Date: _____

Add the titles of each activity chosen to the chart below.

	Content *(0-3 points)*	**Presentation** *(0-2 points)*	*Points Sum*
Choice 1 (top rung): _____			
Points			
Reason for missing points			
Choice 2 (middle rung): _____			
Points			
Reason for missing points			
Choice 3 (bottom rung): _____			
Points			
Reason for missing points			
		Total Points (of 15 maximum)	

Rating Scale			
3	Outstanding	**1**	Needs Improvement
2	Satisfactory	☐	Not Enough Opportunity to Observe

Names of Students

Inquiry Skills										
Observe										
Compare										
Classify/Order										
Gather, Record, Display, or Interpret Data										
Use Numbers										
Communicate										
Plan and Conduct Simple Investigations										
Measure										
Predict										
Infer										
Draw Conclusions										
Use Time/Space Relationships										
Hypothesize										
Formulate or Use Models										
Identify and Control Variables										
Experiment										

Lab and Activity Evaluation

Circle the appropriate number for each criterion. Then add up the circled numbers in each column and record the sum in the subtotals row at the bottom. Add up these subtotals to get the total score.

Graded by _____ Total _____ /100

Behavior	Completely	Mostly	Partially	Poorly
Follows lab procedures carefully and fully	10–9	8–7–6	5–4–3	2–1–0
Wears the required safety equipment and displays knowledge of safety procedures and hazards	10–9	8–7–6	5–4–3	2–1–0
Uses laboratory time productively and stays on task	10–9	8–7–6	5–4–3	2–1–0
Behavior	**Completely**	**Mostly**	**Partially**	**Poorly**
Uses tools, equipment, and materials properly	10–9	8–7–6	5–4–3	2–1–0
Makes quantitative observations carefully, with precision and accuracy	10–9	8–7–6	5–4–3	2–1–0
Uses the appropriate SI units to collect quantitative data	10–9	8–7–6	5–4–3	2–1–0
Records accurate qualitative data during the investigation	10–9	8–7–6	5–4–3	2–1–0
Records measurements and observations in clearly organized tables that have appropriate headings and units	10–9	8–7–6	5–4–3	2–1–0
Works well with partners	10–9	8–7–6	5–4–3	2–1–0
Efficiently and properly solves any minor problems that might occur with materials or procedures	10–9	8–7–6	5–4–3	2–1–0
Subtotals:				

Comments

_____

_____

_____

_____

My Science Portfolio

What Is in My Portfolio	Why I Chose It
1.	
2.	
3.	
4.	
5.	
6.	
7.	

I organized my Science Portfolio this way because _____

_____

_____

_____

_____

Name _____ Date _____

Portfolio Evaluation Checklist

Aspects of Science Literacy	Evidence of Growth
1. Understands science concepts *(Animals, Plants; Earth's Land, Air, Water; Space; Weather; Matter, Motion, Energy)*	_____ _____ _____
2. Uses inquiry skills *(observes, compares, classifies, gathers/ interprets data, communicates, measures, experiments, infers, predicts, draws conclusions)*	_____ _____ _____
3. Thinks critically *(analyzes, synthesizes, evaluates, applies ideas effectively, solves problems)*	_____ _____ _____
4. Displays traits/attitudes of a scientist *(is curious, questioning, persistent, precise, creative, enthusiastic; uses science materials carefully; is concerned for environment)*	_____ _____ _____

Summary of Portfolio Assessment

For This Review			Since Last Review		
Excellent	Good	Fair	Improving	About the Same	Not as Good

Earth's Surface

Choose the letter of the best answer.

1. How would you describe the landscape made by alpine glaciers compared to the landscape made by continental glaciers?

   A. Alpine glaciers form U-shaped valleys, and continental glaciers form V-shaped valleys.

   B. Alpine glaciers form rugged landscapes, and continental glaciers form flat landscapes.

   C. Alpine glaciers form smooth landscapes, and continental glaciers form hilly landscapes.

   D. Alpine glaciers form flattened landscapes, and continental glaciers form uneven landscapes.

2. Sand dunes are formed where wind deposits sand it has been carrying. The following diagram shows a sand dune. The arrows show four different wind directions.

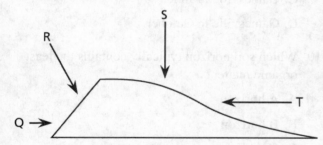

   Which arrow shows the direction in which the wind was blowing to form this sand dune?

   A. arrow Q

   B. arrow R

   C. arrow S

   D. arrow T

3. The continent of Antarctica is covered with an ice sheet. Which part of the Earth system includes the ice sheet?

   A. biosphere

   B. cryosphere

   C. atmosphere

   D. hydrosphere

4. The following diagram shows how sediment is deposited as a fast-flowing river reaches a flatter area of land.

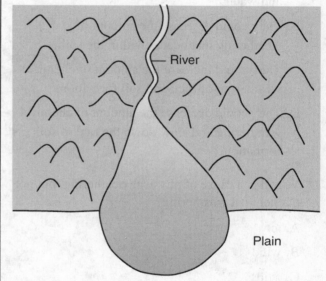

   Which of the following does the diagram show?

   A. river delta

   B. floodplain

   C. alluvial fan

   D. oxbow lake

5. Storms can cause major changes to barrier islands by removing sand from the island. Which of the following would be expected to remove the most sand from a barrier island during a storm?

A. waves depositing debris on the island

B. currents moving sand along the island

C. large waves crashing across the island

D. strong winds blowing across the island

6. Leaves release acids into the soil as they decay. How could decaying leaves affect rock in the soil beneath them?

A. They could expose the rock to wind and water.

B. They could decrease the amount of weathering that occurs within the soil.

C. They could increase the amount of chemical weathering of rock and soil formation.

D. They could decrease the amount of chemical weathering and slow down the rate of soil formation.

7. Which is a cause of physical weathering, but not of chemical weathering?

A. air

B. wind

C. acids

D. water

8. Each layer of the geosphere has a different composition. What element makes up most of Earth's crust?

A. iron

B. nickel

C. oxygen

D. aluminum

9. The graph shows the average monthly rainfall in two Florida cities. Weathering from rain will be the greatest when the amount of rainfall is the highest.

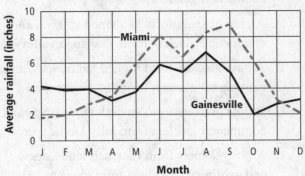

When and where will rainfall cause the **least** weathering?

A. Miami in March

B. Miami in January

C. Gainesville in June

D. Gainesville in October

10. Which soil horizon typically contains the least organic matter?

A. A horizon

B. B horizon

C. C horizon

D. O horizon

Earth's Spheres

Choose the letter of the best answer.

1. Wetlands support many plants, animals, and microscopic organisms. Which part of the Earth system includes the water in wetlands?

   A. the geosphere

   B. the cryosphere

   C. the atmosphere

   D. the hydrosphere

2. The whooping crane is one of the most endangered birds on Earth. Where is the oxygen that whooping cranes breathe located?

   A. in the biosphere

   B. in the geosphere

   C. in the atmosphere

   D. in the hydrosphere

3. Which of these pairs are part of the cryosphere?

   A. rain and snow

   B. glaciers and lakes

   C. permafrost and icebergs

   D. Arctic ice sheet and rainfall

4. Ships encounter surface currents and waves as they travel across the ocean. Surface currents and waves form when energy from the sun causes two of Earth's spheres to interact. Which two spheres interact to produce these waves and currents?

   A. the geosphere and biosphere

   B. the biosphere and hydrosphere

   C. the cryosphere and atmosphere

   D. the atmosphere and hydrosphere

5. Living things in the biosphere interact with other parts of the Earth system to exchange energy. Which picture represents the basic source of energy for the biosphere?

   A.

   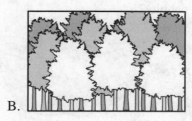
   B.

   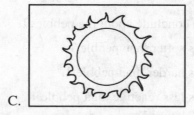
   C.

   D.

Name _____ Date _____

Weathering

Choose the letter of the best answer.

1. What happens to a rock when it is weathered?

    A. It is broken into smaller pieces.

    B. It is moved by wind, air, or water.

    C. It is built up as material is deposited.

    D. It is changed into another type of rock.

2. Zora puts the two pebbles shown in a rock tumbler. The tumbler spins so the rocks bump against each other. When she takes the pebbles out, she discovers that pebble 1 had more abrasion than pebble 2.

    Pebble 1   Pebble 2

    What can she conclude about the pebbles?

    A. Pebble 2 is softer than pebble 1.

    B. Pebble 2 is harder than pebble 1.

    C. Pebble 2 is less reactive than pebble 1.

    D. Pebble 2 is more reactive than pebble 1.

3. What often happens to rocks that undergo chemical weathering?

    A. They form crystals.

    B. They produce acids.

    C. They become stronger.

    D. They crumble more easily.

4. Which are the main causes of crack growth in rocks over time?

    A. plant roots and ice wedging

    B. ice wedging and wind abrasion

    C. animal burrowing and plant roots

    D. animal burrowing and wind abrasion

5. Leaves release acids into the soil as they decay. How could the decaying leaves affect the rocks in the soil underneath them?

    A. They could increase the amount of physical weathering.

    B. They could decrease the amount of physical weathering.

    C. They could increase the amount of chemical weathering.

    D. They could decrease the amount of chemical weathering.

Erosion and Deposition by Water

Choose the letter of the best answer.

1. Marley has a vegetable garden in her yard. During a storm, heavy rain falls. The rain runs over the garden, and some of the soil is washed away. Which term **best** describes this movement of soil from one place to another?

   A. erosion

   B. discharge

   C. deposition

   D. weathering

2. Which statement correctly describes groundwater?

   A. any form of liquid water

   B. water that is not moving

   C. water on Earth's surface

   D. water below Earth's surface

3. While hiking in the mountains, Tanya observed a narrow and steep valley with a stream at the bottom of it. What **most likely** caused the valley to first form?

   A. an earthquake

   B. running water

   C. a rock landslide

   D. erosion by wind

4. Rhianna has a stream flowing through her farm. The sediment flowing in the stream is usually fine sand. After a storm, the sediment is a mixture of fine sand, coarse sand, and pebbles. What would Rhianna most likely observe?

   A. no erosion after a storm

   B. no erosion before a storm

   C. a lower rate of erosion after a storm

   D. a higher rate of erosion after a storm

5. The alluvial fan shown in the following illustration formed as sediment began to drop out from a stream that could no longer carry all of its sediment.

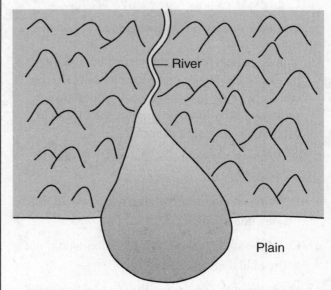

Which statement best explains why the stream could no longer carry all its sediment?

   A. The volume of water was too high.

   B. The slope of the land was too great.

   C. The speed of the water was too slow.

   D. The width of the stream was too small.

Erosion and Deposition by Wind, Ice, and Gravity

Choose the letter of the best answer.

1. Which of the following is a type of mass movement caused by gravity?

   A. dune

   B. loess

   C. glacier

   D. mudslide

2. Loess is a very valuable resource. What characteristic of loess makes it so valuable?

   A. Loess is rich in minerals.

   B. Loess contains bits of rock.

   C. Loess does not erode easily.

   D. Loess is very difficult to find.

3. When glaciers retreat, they leave behind huge blocks of ice. When these ice blocks melt, they can form kettle lakes. Why is it important for sediment to build up around the ice blocks in order for kettle lakes to form?

   A. Without the sediment, the water in the lake would dry up.

   B. Without the sediment, the water would not stay contained.

   C. Without the sediment, vegetation would not be able to grow.

   D. Without the sediment, the ice blocks would not warm enough to melt.

4. The landform shown in the following picture can be found on every continent; they are even found in Africa.

   What conditions are necessary for this landform to form?

   A. It must be below freezing and very dry.

   B. It must be cold, and more snow must fall than melts.

   C. It must be mild, and there must be lots of precipitation.

   D. It must be below freezing, and more snow must melt than falls.

5. The tallest sand dunes in North America are found in Great Sand Dunes National Park and Preserve in Colorado. These dunes were formed from the sand at the bottom of a dry lake bed. Which of the following agents is most likely responsible for the formation of the sand dunes?

   A. ice

   B. wind

   C. water

   D. gravity

Soil Formation

Choose the letter of the best answer.

1. Susan rubs two rocks together. One of the rocks wears away to form small particles. What would most likely happen if this rock continues to break into small pieces after Susan puts the rocks back on the ground?

   A. The pieces may become part of the soil.

   B. The pieces may become part of the bedrock.

   C. The pieces may become part of the ice wedging process.

   D. The pieces may become part of the organic matter in the soil.

2. Gopher tortoises live on dry land. They live in large holes that they dig in the soil. Which statement gives the best explanation of how this behavior aids in soil formation?

   A. It hardens the soil, allowing less water to reach the rocks underground.

   B. It erodes the soil by moving it from underneath the ground to above ground.

   C. It loosens and mixes the soil, increasing air in the soil and the ability to drain water.

   D. It causes weathering of the rocks, as the tortoise breaks the rocks into smaller pieces.

3. Which of the following describes how microorganisms influence the chemical characteristics of soil?

   A. They loosen and mix the soil by digging burrows underground.

   B. They add inorganic material to the soil by weathering rocks on Earth's surface.

   C. They add moisture to the soil by creating pores through which water can move.

   D. They add organic material to the soil by breaking down the remains of plants and animals.

4. Examine the soil profile below. Note there are many ground cover plants and a tree with deep roots.

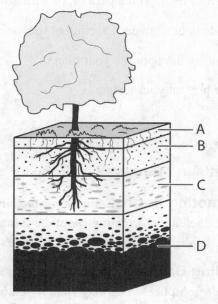

   Which soil horizon is primarily responsible for this soil's fertility?

   A. Horizon A, because it contains humus and other organic nutrients that plants need.

   B. Horizon B, because plant roots can grow down into the smaller rock fragments.

   C. Horizon C, because most of the groundwater is stored in this horizon.

   D. Horizon D, because it is the parent rock that breaks up to form soil.

5. What is humus?

   A. spaces between soil particles through which water and air can move

   B. weathered sediment broken down by atmospheric forces on Earth's surface

   C. dark, organic material formed in soil from the decayed remains of plants and animals

   D. a loose mixture of rock fragments, organic material, water, and air that can support the growth of vegetation

Earth's Spheres

Choose Your Meal: *Earth's System and Earth's Spheres*
Complete the activities to show what you've learned about the Earth system, Earth's spheres, and Earth's energy budget.

1. Work on your own, with a partner, or with a small group.

2. Choose one item from each section of the menu, with an optional dessert. Check your choices.

3. Have your teacher approve your plan.

4. Submit or present your results.

Appetizers

_____ **What's in a Sphere?** Write a poem about Earth's spheres. Include all spheres in your poem.

_____ **Promoting Earth** Compose a brochure that encourages an alien species to move to the planet Earth. Include information about the Earth system and the ways living things, nonliving things, and Earth's spheres work together to make it a good planet to live on. Include an illustration of Earth.

_____ **Peeling Back the Layers** Create a PowerPoint presentation in which you describe the layers of Earth's geosphere. You may want to feature one layer on each slide. Include pictures or diagrams.

Main Dish

_____ **Earth's Description** Write a description from Earth's point of view. Have Earth give an overview of its systems and give examples of the ways the systems work together.

Side Dishes

_____ **Fan Club** Suppose you run the atmosphere's fan club. Design a Web page for your club. Include information on the atmosphere's composition and size, and on how it helps us.

_____ **Job Description** Imagine you are hiring an accountant to balance Earth's energy budget. Write a job description, explaining what needs to be balanced and why it is so important.

Desserts (optional)

_____ **Where's the Water?** Create a poster of Earth's hydrosphere. Include all the parts of the hydrosphere including water underground and in clouds. Label the parts.

_____ **Composing Questions** Write a quiz about the cryosphere. Include at least five questions or activities on your quiz and include an answer key.

Weathering

Take Your Pick: *Weathering*
Weathering can be either physical or chemical. These activities
will help you learn more about both.

1. Work on your own, with a partner, or with a small group.

2. Choose one or more items for a total of at least 10 points. Check your choices.

3. Have your teacher approve your plan.

4. Submit or present your results.

2 Points

_____ **Crossword Puzzle** Make a crossword puzzle that includes the different agents of weathering. Use definitions and descriptions of the specific types of weathering caused by the agent.

_____ **Illustration of Agents** Weathering occurs through many different agents. Make an illustration of a landscape that includes several agents of weathering.

5 Points

_____ **Wanted Poster** Chemical weathering occurs through many different agents. Make a Wanted poster identifying these agents. You poster could be for a criminal (Agent Wanted), a star agent (Star Agent Wanted), or jobs needed to make the weathering occur (Jobs Wanted). Include pictures and descriptions about how each causes weathering.

_____ **Model** Using recycled materials, make a model of an area that has experienced at least two kinds of chemical weathering. Be sure to include labeled descriptions of how the weathering occurred.

_____ **Quiz** Write your own quiz on physical weathering. Make sure you ask questions about agents of physical weathering, how the physical weathering occurs, and what the results of physical weathering are. Include an answer key.

_____ **Newspaper Article** Invent a newsworthy example of chemical weathering. Then write a newspaper article about it. As background for your article, explore other types of weathering, too.

8 Points

_____ **Interview with a Landform** Write a interview between you and an outcrop of bedrock that has experienced chemical and physical weathering. Ask the outcrop about its weathering from the past, and what it expects in the future. Include a picture of the outcrop showing the weathering it has experienced.

_____ **Timeline** Create an imagined timeline of physical and chemical weathering that has occurred to a material. Show what the material looks like at different points along the timeline.

Erosion and Deposition by Water

Alternative Assessment

Mix and Match: *Pathways of Erosion and Deposition*
Mix and match ideas to show what you've learned about erosion and deposition.

1. Work on your own, with a partner, or with a small group.

2. Choose one information source from Column A, two topics from Column B, and one option from Column C. Check your choices.

3. Have your teacher approve your plan.

4. Submit or present your results.

A. Choose One Information Source	B. Choose Two Things to Analyze	C. Choose One Way to Communicate Analysis
___ photograph of a landform	___ pathway, size, and speed of water	___ diagram or illustration
___ observations of a stream or coast	___ origin and destination of material	___ colors, arrows, or symbols marked on a visual, with a key
___ an aerial photograph of an alluvial fan	___ past history	___ model, such as drawings or simulations with sand or clay
___ observations of a local farm	___ future prediction	
___ website describing national parks	___ speed of landform change and why	___ booklet, such as a field guide, travel brochure, playbook, or set of instructions
___ descriptions or photographs of a flood		___ game
___ topographical map		___ story, song, or poem, with supporting details
___ descriptions or photographs of a coastline before and after a big storm		___ skit, chant, or dance, with supporting details
___ geological map		___ Multimedia presentation
_____		___ mathematical depiction
		_____

Erosion and Deposition by Wind, Ice, and Gravity

Tic-Tac-Toe: *Make a Board Game*

You are designing a board game in which players must explain forms of erosion and deposition situations. You must test your game's questions before your game is manufactured.

1. Work on your own, with a partner, or with a small group.

2. Choose three quick activities from the game. Check the boxes you plan to complete. They must form a straight line in any direction.

3. Have your teacher approve your plan.

4. Do each activity, and turn in your results.

__ **Desert Pavement**	__ **Dunes**	__ **Loess**
Your game includes an area of harsh desert pavement. Game questions: What does desert pavement look like? Why does it look this way?	Your players must cross areas of dunes. Game questions: Do dunes stay the same over time? Why or why not?	In your game, there is an area of loess your players must go around. Game question: How did this loess get so fertile?
__ **Alpine Glacier**	__ **Continental Glacier**	__ **Glacial Drift**
Players must cross an area with an alpine glacier and all of the features it can create. Game questions: What features can an alpine glacier create? How does this happen?	A continental glacier covers part of your board. Game questions: How big can a continental glacier be? Where can you find a continental glacier? How is a continental glacier different than an alpine glacier?	Glacial drift makes some areas of your game board difficult to move across. Game question: How did all this material get here?
__ **Creep**	__ **Rock Fall and Landslides**	__ **Mudflows and Lahars**
Players can only cross slopes experiencing creep if they explain what it is. Game question: What is creep?	Rock falls and landslides form some difficult terrain for players. Game question: What conditions are perfect for creating rock falls and landslides?	Hazardous areas of your game include mudflows and lahars. Game questions: Why is a mudflow dangerous? Where can a mudflow occur? What is the difference between a mudflow and a lahar?

Soil Formation

Mix and Match: *All About Soil*

Mix and match ideas to show what you've learned about soil and how it forms.

1. Work on your own, with a partner, or with a small group.

2. Choose one information source from Column A, two topics from Column B, and one option from Column C. Check your choices.

3. Have your teacher approve your plan.

4. Submit or present your results.

A. Choose One or More Information Sources	B. Choose Two or More Things to Analyze	C. Choose One Way to Communicate Analysis
____ direct observations of soil in a natural environment	____ soil horizons	____ realistic illustration
____ direct observation of modified soil, such as from a garden or a potted plant	____ soil characteristics (texture, color, moisture, organic matter, fertility)	____ schematic diagram with a key
____ observations of soil from a photograph, video, or similar source	____ soil chemistry	____ model
____ records of observations of soil, such as from a naturalist's journal or a geological survey	____ formation, including possible parent rock or transport	____ informational booklet, such as a field guide
	____ actions of living things	____ multimedia presentation
_____		_____

Weathering

Purpose In this activity, students will use sandpaper and wood to model differential weathering.

Time Period 45–60 minutes

Preparation Pine wood scraps with knots may be found at a local hardware store, lumberyard, or school wood shop. Equip each activity station with the necessary materials.

Safety Tips Have students review all safety icons before beginning this activity. This activity should be performed in an area free from drafts. In addition to safety goggles, lab aprons, and gloves, students should wear disposable filter masks to protect their lungs from sawdust.

Teaching Strategies This activity works best with students working in pairs. You may choose to have students repeat this experiment with different grades of sandpaper to model different climatic conditions. A coarser grade of sandpaper will correspond to a warmer, moister climate. A finer grade will correspond to a drier climate.

Scoring Rubric

Possible points	Performance indicators
0–30	Lab technique
0–30	Quality and clarity of observations
0–40	Explanation of observations

Weathering

Objective

The weathering of rocks on Earth's surface can be compared to the action of sandpaper on wood.
In this activity, you will model weathering using sandpaper and wood.

Know the Score!

As you work through this activity, keep in mind that you will be earning a grade for the following:

- how well you work with materials and equipment (30%)
- how well you state your observations (30%)
- how well you explain your observations (40%)

Materials and Equipment

- clock
- gloves, cloth
- mask, filter
- newspaper

- ruler
- sandpaper, coarse
- tape, masking
- wood, pine, piece containing a knot

Safety Information

- Wear protective eyewear, cloth gloves, and a disposable filter mask.

Procedure

1. Describe the wood. Include information about texture, color, and how the knotty wood is different from the rest of the wood.

   _____

   _____

   _____

   _____

2. Tape a sheet of newspaper over your desk to protect it during this experiment.

3. Draw a 5 × 10 cm rectangle on the wood so that half of the rectangle contains plain wood and the other half contains knotty wood.

4. Use the sandpaper to sand the wood inside the rectangle for 10 minutes. Sand the rectangle using even pressure. Compare the change in the plain wood and the knotty wood. Record your observations below.

_____

_____

_____

_____

Analysis

5. How is the action of sandpaper on wood similar to the weathering of rocks on Earth's surface?

_____

_____

_____

6. In this activity, which materials are worn down? Explain.

_____

_____

_____

_____

7. How could you model chemical weathering using the piece of wood? What would be a limitation of such an experiment?

_____

_____

_____

Unit 1: Earth's Surface

Vocabulary

Fill in each blank with the term that best completes the following sentences.

1. _____ is the dark, organic-rich material formed as a top layer in soil from the decayed remains of plants and animals.

2. The process by which rocks break down as a result of chemical reactions is called

   _____.

3. The fan-shaped mass of sediment deposited by a stream into an ocean or a lake is called a

   _____.

4. The rock material deposited by glaciers as they melt and retreat is called _____.

5. The _____ is the part of Earth where life exists and extends from the deep ocean floors up into the lower atmosphere.

Key Concepts

Read each question below, and circle the best answer.

6. Which term describes the ability a soil has to support plant growth?

   A. chemistry

   B. fertility

   C. texture

   D. pore space

7. What are two processes that result in rocks being broken down into smaller pieces?

   A. sunlight and glacial melting

   B. chemical weathering and physical weathering

   C. chemical weathering and deposition

   D. physical weathering and humus

8. This diagram shows a landform called an alluvial fan.

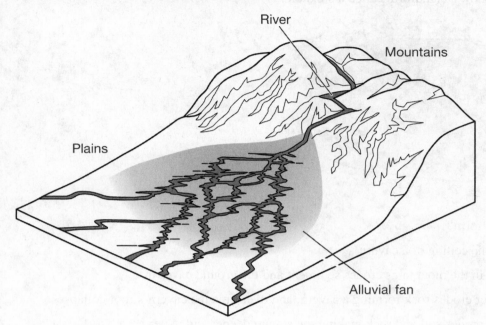

How does an alluvial fan form?

A. It forms where a stream enters an ocean or lake, slows down, and deposits sediments there over time.

B. It forms from a stream overflowing and depositing sediments.

C. It forms where part of a meandering stream is cut off.

D. It forms where a stream reaches a flat area of land, slows down, and deposits sediments there over time.

9. While walking along a seashore, Antonio determined that the shore has been affected by stormy seas and rough waves. What did Antonio observe?

A. The beach was sandy.   C. The beach was rocky.

B. There were sandbars.   D. There was a sea stack.

10. Landslides, rockfalls, and creep are examples of erosion and deposition by which erosion agent?

A. gravity   C. oxidation

B. solar energy   D. wind

11. The diagram below shows a landform called a sinkhole.

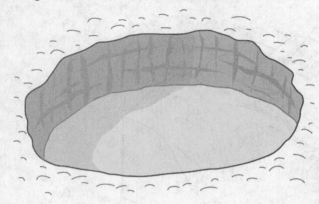

How does a sinkhole form?

A. Stalactites erode the ceiling of a cavern.

B. A flowing stream in the mountains erodes sediment and the ground caves in.

C. Underground water erodes rock forming a cavern, and over time the cavern's roof collapses.

D. A flowing stream erodes soil and rock making the stream deeper and wider.

12. A glacier is a large mass of moving ice. What conditions are necessary for a glacier to form?

A. The weather must be below freezing and very dry.

B. The weather must be below freezing, and more snow must fall than melt.

C. The weather must be mild, and there must be a lot of precipitation.

D. The weather must be below freezing, and more snow must melt than fall.

Critical Thinking
Answer the following questions in the space provided.

13. Explain whether water is a cause of either chemical weathering, physical weathering, or both.

_____

_____

_____

_____

_____

14. Below is a diagram of the soil profile of three layers of soil.

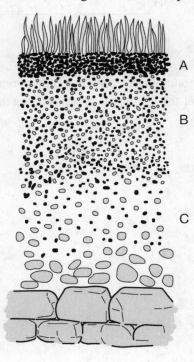

A

B

C

Describe the characteristics and properties of the three layers of soil.

_____

_____

_____

_____

_____

Connect ESSENTIAL QUESTIONS

Lessons 3 and 4

Answer the following question in the space provided.

15. How can water and gravity work together to erode soil, sediment, and rock? Give two examples.

_____

_____

_____

Explain how water deposits soil, sediment, and rock. Give two examples. _____

_____

_____

_____

Earth's Surface

Key Concepts
Choose the letter of the best answer.

1. A river starts as a steep channel in the mountains. It then leaves the mountains and enters a flatter area of land. It meanders across a plain and then enters the ocean. Which of the following actions causes the deposition of sand at a delta?

   A. river water slowing as it enters the ocean

   B. salt water and fresh water mixing together

   C. ocean waves transporting sand toward land

   D. ocean water slowing as it reaches the coast

2. What can cause granite to break down into soil over time?

   A. rain and wind

   B. sand deposition

   C. heat from magma

   D. pressure underground

3. The graph shows the average acidity of precipitation for various locations in the United States in 2007. The lower the pH value is for a substance, the more acidic that substance is.

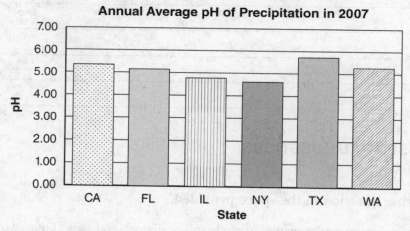

Based on the data in the graph, if each state had about the same amount of precipitation in 2007, which state would have had the highest rate of chemical weathering?

   A. Texas (TX)

   B. California (CA)

   C. New York (NY)

   D. Washington (WA)

4. Canyons, caverns, channels, and valleys all form because of erosion by water. Which landform listed is **mainly** formed because of erosion by groundwater?

   A. a broad valley

   B. a narrow canyon

   C. a human-made channel

   D. an underground cavern

5. Emily used a tray filled with dirt as a model of a stream. Emily poured water into the top of the tray and observed how much erosion happened. Emily then increased the slope of the tray and repeated the experiment.

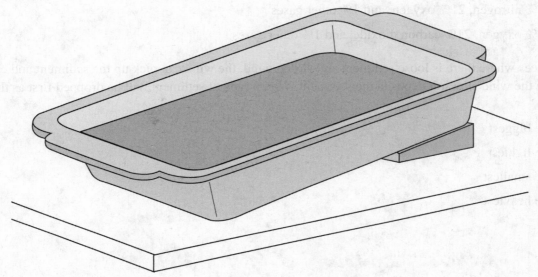

   What would happen when the slope of the tray increased?

   A. The speed of the water and the amount of erosion would increase.

   B. The speed of the water and the amount of erosion would decrease.

   C. The speed of the water would increase, while the amount of erosion would decrease.

   D. The speed of the water would decrease, while the amount of erosion would increase.

6. Which of the following is the source of humus found in soil?

   A. bedrock

   B. B horizon

   C. parent rock

   D. plants and animals

7. Which is an example of abrasion of a rock?

   A. a color change due to exposure to air

   B. a shape change due to exposure to wind

   C. a hole forming due to a reaction with water

   D. a layer falling off due to a lessening of pressure

8. What is the composition of Earth's atmosphere?

   A. 78% nitrogen and 22% water vapor

   B. 78% oxygen and 22% carbon dioxide

   C. 78% nitrogen, 21% oxygen, and 1% other gases

   D. 78% oxygen, 21% carbon dioxide, and 1% other gases

9. In places where there is loose sediment and strong wind, the wind can pick up the sediment and carry it. When the wind slows, it deposits the sediment. Which type of sediment will be dropped first as the wind slows?

   A. the biggest

   B. the lightest

   C. the smallest

   D. the heaviest

10. The picture below shows the layers of the geosphere.

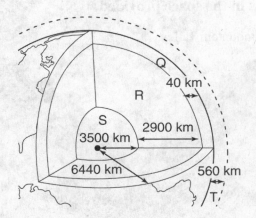

What is the order of the layers of the geosphere when starting from Earth's center and moving outward?

A. core, crust, mantle

B. core, mantle, crust

C. mantle, core, atmosphere

D. atmosphere, crust, mantle

11. Landslides, rockfalls, and mudslides are responsible for both erosion and deposition. What force is mainly responsible for the erosion and deposition that happens in landslides, rockfalls, and mudslides?

A. ice

B. wind

C. gravity

D. temperature

12. Granite has only recently been exposed at a location on Earth's surface. How will this most likely affect the soil that will eventually form at this location?

A. The soil will have a thick layer of humus in the A horizon.

B. The soil will contain many of the same minerals as the granite has.

C. The soil will consist of thin horizons compared to other types of soils.

D. The soil will be made of mostly rock material instead of organic matter.

Critical Thinking

Answer the following questions in the space provided.

13. The following picture shows a mountain valley.

Explain how you would expect this valley to look after a glacier moves through it. Explain how the glacier changes the valley.

_____

_____

_____

_____

Extended Response
Answer the following questions in the space provided.

14. List four of Earth's spheres that contain water, and identify one way that water is stored in each.

_____

_____

_____

_____

_____

_____

_____

_____

Earth's Surface

Key Concepts
Choose the letter of the best answer.

1. A river starts as a steep channel in the mountains. It then leaves the mountains and enters a flatter area of land. It meanders across a plain and then enters the ocean. At which point would the river described form a delta?

    A. when the river enters the ocean

    B. when the river is in the mountains

    C. when the river leaves the mountains

    D. when the river meanders across a plain

2. What can cause granite to break down into soil over time?

    A. heat from magma

    B. burrowing organisms

    C. pressure underground

    D. exposure to plant acids

3. The graph shows the average acidity for various locations in the United States in 2007. The lower the pH value is for a substance, the more acidic that substance is.

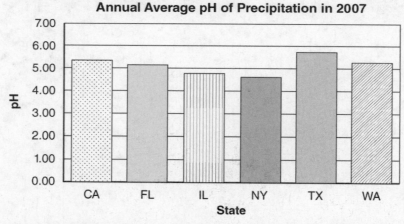

If both New York (NY) and Washington (WA) had about the same amount of precipitation in 2007, what can you conclude about the amount of chemical weathering that would have happened in each state?

A. Neither location will experience much chemical weathering.

B. The amount of chemical weathering should be about the same.

C. The chemical weathering will be greater in Washington than in New York.

D. The chemical weathering will be greater in New York than in Washington.

4. Which of the following best describes how erosion by groundwater might create a landform?

   A. Slightly acidic water dissolves certain rocks underground to form a cavern.

   B. A stream flowing through a plain gradually wears away the rock and soil to form a valley.

   C. Waves crashing against a rocky shoreline cause parts of the cliff to break away and produce a sea cave.

   D. River water slows down as it approaches the ocean and deposits sediment that builds up to form a delta.

5. A student made a model of a river using a tray filled with sand. The student poured a cup of water into the top of the tray. The student then poured a bucket of water into the top of the tray.

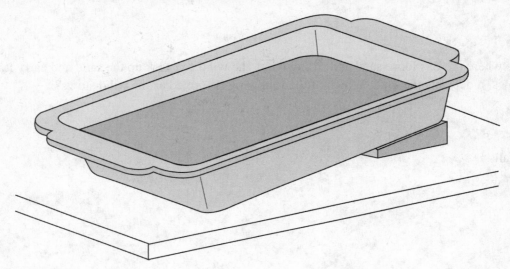

   What would most likely be observed?

   A. The cup of water would cause more erosion than the bucket of water.

   B. The bucket of water would cause more erosion than the cup of water.

   C. The cup of water and the bucket of water would not cause any erosion.

   D. The cup of water and the bucket of water would cause the same erosion.

6. In which of the following soil layers is humus mostly found?

   A. A horizon

   B. B horizon

   C. C horizon

   D. D horizon

7. Which of the following typically results from abrasion of a rock?

   A. a change in size

   B. deposition of sediment

   C. a different surface color

   D. movement to a new location

8. What is the nitrogen content of Earth's atmosphere?

   A. 1%

   B. 21%

   C. 78%

   D. 99%

9. In places where there is loose sand and strong wind, the wind can pick up the sand and carry it. When the wind slows, it deposits the sand. Which of the following is formed as the wind slows?

   A. dunes

   B. glaciers

   C. rockfalls

   D. mudflows

10. The picture below shows the layers of the geosphere.

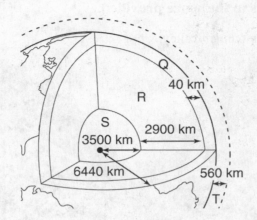

What is the order of the layers of the geosphere when starting from Earth's surface and moving inward?

A. crust, mantle, core

B. core, mantle, crust

C. mantle, core, atmosphere

D. atmosphere, crust, mantle

11. Landslides, rockfalls, and mudslides are responsible for both erosion and deposition. What condition is most likely to trigger a mudslide?

A. ice

B. rain

C. wind

D. temperature

12. Granite has only recently been exposed at a location on Earth's surface. What will need to happen first in order for soil to eventually form in this location?

A. A thick layer of humus must form on top of the granite.

B. The granite must be broken into smaller pieces by weathering processes.

C. Erosion by wind and water must move pieces of granite to other locations.

D. Microorganisms must begin to break down the remains of plants and animals.

Critical Thinking
Answer the following questions in the space provided.

13. The following picture shows a mountain valley.

Draw a picture of how you would expect this valley to look after a glacier moves through it.

Explain how your drawing shows how the glacier changed the valley.

_____

_____

_____

_____

_____

Extended Response
Answer the following questions in the space provided.

14. List two of Earth's spheres that contain water and also interact with the hydrosphere. For each of the spheres you list, explain one way that water is transferred between that sphere and the hydrosphere.

_____

_____

_____

_____

_____

_____

_____

_____

Earth's History

Choose the letter of the best answer.

1. Which of the following is evidence that supports the idea of uniformitarianism?

   A. Flooding causes a higher than normal erosion rate during wet years.

   B. Rates of soil erosion are much lower during droughts that last several years.

   C. Rates of soil erosion are approximately the same over a period of many years.

   D. Flash floods cause erosion by washing away the top layer of soil in wet years.

2. Scientists have determined an approximate age for Earth. To do this, they tested samples of meteorites, rock from the moon, and rocks from other parts of the solar system. Which method could be used to determine the age of these samples?

   A. index fossil dating

   B. radiocarbon dating

   C. uranium-lead dating

   D. sedimentary rock dating

3. The table below shows the half-lives of three isotopes.

Isotope	Half-Life
uranium-238	4.5 billion years
uranium-235	704 billion years
potassium-40	1.3 billion years

   Which statement best explains why these isotopes can be used to date rocks?

   A. They are all rare isotopes.

   B. They all decay at set rates.

   C. They are all large isotopes.

   D. They are all stable over time.

4. A team of scientists is searching for specimens to understand how Earth's climate has changed in the past. The black boxes in the figure below show where this team has drilled to obtain such specimens.

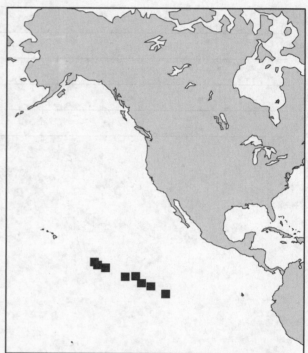

   What were these scientists drilling for?

   A. ice cores

   B. surface landforms

   C. sea-floor sediments

   D. fossils preserved in amber

5. Julia has two samples of rocks for which she wants to find the absolute ages. She has a sample of sandstone and a sample of granite. Which statement explains why she can more easily date the granite sample?

   A. The granite is older.

   B. The granite is igneous.

   C. The granite is younger.

   D. The granite is sedimentary.

6. Florida was once part of Gondwanaland, which was a supercontinent that later divided into Africa and South America. Which statement best describes this process?

   A. A volcanic eruption likely caused Gondwanaland to divide.

   B. The continents have been moving throughout Earth's history.

   C. Weathering and erosion eventually broke Gondwanaland apart.

   D. Africa and South America go through cycles of dividing and colliding.

7. According to the fossil record, when did the dinosaurs become extinct?

   A. at the end of the Mesozoic Era

   B. at the end of the Paleozoic Era

   C. at the start of the Mesozoic Era

   D. at the start of the Paleozoic Era

8. What is the law of superposition?

   A. Igneous rock is older than nearby sedimentary rock, which is older than nearby metamorphic rock.

   B. A sedimentary rock layer in its original position is older than the layers above it and younger than the layers below it.

   C. Metamorphic rock is older than nearby sedimentary rock because sedimentary rock is deposited before metamorphic rock forms.

   D. The exact age of a sedimentary rock layer can be found using the layers above and below it, even if the layers are not in their original positions.

9. Many fossils are found only during certain periods in the geologic record. Scientists use these fossils to determine the relative ages of rock layers. The diagram shows relative ages of four fossils.

Fossil E	Fossil F	Fossil G	Fossil H

Period 1	Period 2	Period 3	Period 4	Period 5	Period 6	Period 7

→ Increasing age

Which statement is true of a rock layer that contains fossil F?

   A. It could also contain fossil G.

   B. It was formed in periods 1, 2, and 3.

   C. It is older than the rock layers that contain fossil H.

   D. It is younger than the rock layers formed in period 4.

10. How does the law of crosscutting relationships explain the age of a fault caused by an earthquake?

   A. The fault is older than the rocks above it.

   B. The fault is younger than the rocks above it.

   C. The fault is older than the rocks it cuts through.

   D. The fault is younger than the rocks it cuts through.

Geologic Change over Time

Choose the letter of the best answer.

1. The figure below shows an example of a geologic change that supports the principle of uniformitarianism.

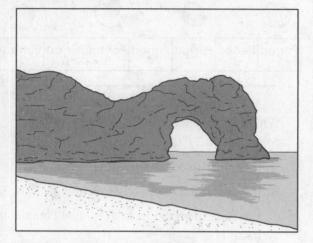

   What geologic change is shown in the figure?

   A. erosion

   B. abrasion

   C. volcanism

   D. deposition

2. Earth's surface features slowly change over time. For example, sharp, jagged mountain ranges become lower and more rounded over time. What factor or factors is/are responsible for this change in their shape?

   A. deposition

   B. weathering and erosion

   C. movement of continents

   D. collisions between continental plates

3. In 1897, a British scientist proposed that Earth was between 20 and 400 million years old. Based on radiometric dating, scientists now propose a different age for Earth. Based on the most current radiometric dating data, about how old is Earth?

   A. 40 billion years old

   B. 20 billion years old

   C. 4.6 billion years old

   D. 4.6 million years old

4. Florida State University has a large collection of ice cores taken from the Antarctic. What can scientists learn by studying these ice cores?

   A. history of Earth's climate

   B. how continents have moved

   C. how new species have evolved

   D. major changes that have taken place on Earth's surface

5. Trace fossils are much more common than body fossils. Which of the following best explains why trace fossils are more common?

   A. Trace fossils take less time to form.

   B. Body fossils require soft sediment to form.

   C. An organism is more likely to live on soft sediment where trace fossils form.

   D. A single animal can leave thousands of traces in its lifetime but will leave only one body when it dies.

Relative Dating

Choose the letter of the best answer.

1. Which of these choices is an example of the way a geologist would use relative dating?

   A. determining the minerals that make up rocks

   B. placing rock layers in order of oldest to youngest

   C. classifying rocks as igneous, sedimentary, or metamorphic

   D. using radioactive isotopes to determine the exact age of rock samples

2. The following diagram shows rock layers that are cut by a fault and two bodies of rock (rock 1 and rock 2).

   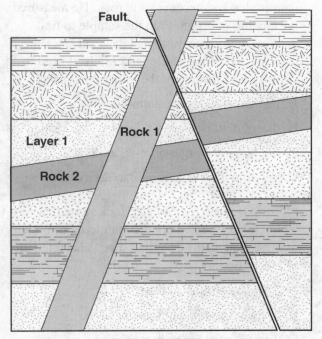

   What are the relative ages of the features in order of oldest to youngest?

   A. fault, rock 1, rock 2, layer 1

   B. layer 1, rock 2, rock 1, fault

   C. rock 2, layer 1, rock 1, fault

   D. fault, rock 2, layer 1, rock 1

3. Fossils are the preserved remains or traces of plants and animals that have lived on Earth throughout Earth's history. How does the fossil record of animals compare to animals that exist today?

   A. Animals in the fossil record are the same as animals that exist today.

   B. Animals in the fossil record are ancestors of animals that exist today.

   C. Animals in the fossil record have no similarities to animals that exist today.

   D. Animals in the fossil record are more complex than animals that exist today.

4. A geologist is studying three layers of sedimentary rock in an area. The layers have not shifted from their original positions. The geologist records the relative ages of the rocks. The bottom layer is listed as the oldest. The top layer is listed as the youngest. What did the geologist use to determine the relative ages of the rocks?

   A. mineral content

   B. radioactive decay

   C. the law of superposition

   D. the principle of unconformity

5. What is a geologic column?

   A. a rock structure that is shaped like a column

   B. a body of rock that cuts through sedimentary rock layers

   C. a group of rock layers that are taken out of the ground to study

   D. a group of rock layers that are placed in order of their relative ages

Absolute Dating

Choose the letter of the best answer.

1. A student drew the diagram below to show one kind of radioactive decay.

    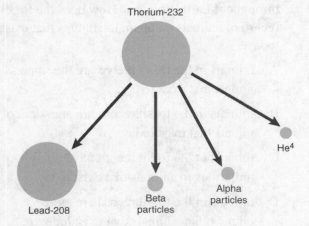

    Thorium-232

    He⁴

    Lead-208

    Beta particles

    Alpha particles

    Which of the following statements correctly describes this decay process?

    A. Thorium-232 and lead-208 are both parent isotopes.

    B. Thorium-232 and lead-208 are both daughter isotopes.

    C. Thorium-232 is the parent isotope, and lead-208 is the daughter isotope.

    D. Thorium-232 is the daughter isotope, and lead-208 is the parent isotope.

2. Sandra is making a poster of Earth's geologic history. She wants to include a timeline on her poster. Which date should Sandra use at the beginning of her timeline, to show Earth's formation in the solar system?

    A. 3.5 million years ago

    B. 700 million years ago

    C. 4.6 billion years ago

    D. 12 billion years ago

3. Which of these choices is the best definition of absolute dating?

    A. finding the age of an object compared to other objects

    B. measuring the age of an object in years using any method

    C. determining the amount of a radioactive isotope in an object

    D. determining the age of a rock layer by studying the fossils present

4. To determine when a volcano erupted, Michael used a sample of a mineral that formed when the lava cooled and became solid rock. He measured the amount of argon-40 in the sample to find how much potassium-40 had decayed since the rock formed. What else would Michael need to know to find the age of the mineral in years?

    A. the half-life of potassium-40

    B. the amount of energy released

    C. the mass of a potassium-40 atom

    D. the time it takes argon-40 to decay

5. Index fossils are used to date rock strata that would otherwise be very difficult to date. Which of these statements describes a key characteristic of index fossils?

    A. They are similar to other fossils.

    B. They existed in a unique location.

    C. They existed for a short span of time.

    D. They are present in very small numbers.

The Geologic Time Scale

Choose the letter of the best answer.

1. In what way are eras different from periods?

   A. They are longer spans of time.

   B. They are subdivided into epochs.

   C. They have a longer duration than eons.

   D. They have boundaries marked by mass extinctions.

2. The geologic time scale is divided by several different spans of time. Which of the following divisions of time are all eras?

   A. Cretaceous, Jurassic, Triassic

   B. Paleocene, Eocene, Oligocene

   C. Cenozoic, Mesozoic, Paleozoic

   D. Precambrian, Cambrian, Devonian

3. What is the main criterion that scientists use to decide where to place the boundaries between the major divisions of the geologic time scale?

   A. major changes in the structure of Earth's layers

   B. major changes that occur in the solar system

   C. major changes that are recorded in the fossil record

   D. major changes in the arrangement of the continents

4. Which of the following statements correctly defines geology?

   A. It is the scientific study of the history of Earth and the processes that shape it.

   B. It is the scientific study of the history of the solar system and the processes that shape it.

   C. It is the scientific study of the development of life on Earth and the processes that change it.

   D. It is the scientific study of the structure of Earth's atmosphere and the processes that change it.

5. During the Paleozoic Era, the Appalachian Mountains of eastern North America began to form. The map below shows Earth's continents at about 50 million years ago, after the breakup of the supercontinent Pangaea. Since then, North America has continued to move farther away from Africa and Eurasia.

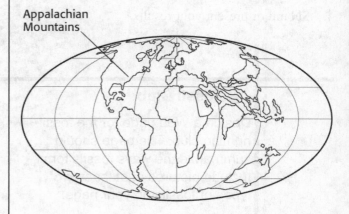

Appalachian Mountains

Based on this map, what most likely caused the Appalachian Mountains to form?

A. a collision between North America and Africa

B. volcanic eruptions in North America and Africa

C. the spreading apart of North America and Africa

D. widespread earthquakes in North America and Africa

Geologic Change Over Time

Climb the Ladder: *Fossil Hunters*

You are a member of a local fossil-hunting club that enjoys searching for different types of fossils and learning about Earth's geologic history.

1. Work on your own, with a partner, or with a small group.

2. Choose one item from each rung of the ladder. Check your choices.

3. Have your teacher approve your plan.

4. Submit or present your results.

__ Fossil Club Design a Web page for the fossil-hunting club. The page should summarize the ways fossils form. Include pictures of at least two types of fossils on your page.	**__ Club Headquarters** Design a poster for your club's headquarters. On the poster, describe how sedimentary rock can give scientists information about Earth's past. Include at least two images of sedimentary rocks on your poster.
__ Climate Quiz Compose a quiz to test your club members' knowledge about the materials that tell us about Earth's climate history. Include at least five questions on your quiz. The answers can be multiple-choice, short answer, or true/false.	**__ Climate Clues** Imagine that members of your club found some fossils. Many of the fossils are of tropical palm fronds and ferns. Present a news report about your club's findings. In your report, explain what these fossils might indicate about the climate in the past.
__ The Aging Earth Imagine that your club has been asked to speak at a conference about Earth's age. Present a speech about uniformitarianism. In your speech, define uniformitarianism and explain how it relates to determining Earth's age.	**__ Move Along** Imagine your club is going to perform a short play about the break-up of Pangaea. Write the script. Start your script about 200 million years ago, and include evidence that the continents have been drifting apart since that time.

Relative Dating

Choose Your Meal: *Relative Dating*
Complete the activities to show what you've learned about relative dating.

1. Work on your own, with a partner, or with a small group.

2. Choose one item from each section of the menu, with an optional dessert. Check your choices.

3. Have your teacher approve your plan.

4. Submit or present your results.

Appetizers

_____ **Sedimentary Summary** Design a pamphlet that describes the process in which sedimentary rock layers are formed. Include at least two illustrations of undisturbed sedimentary rock layers.

_____ **This Just In!** Present a news report in which you identify and describe a section of sedimentary rock that has been disturbed. Include information about how the rock was disturbed and how scientists can use other clues to help them date the disturbed rock correctly.

Main Dish

_____ **Relative Dating** Write a poem, report, or Website about relative dating. In your work, define relative dating, explain the methods scientists use to conduct relative dating, and add illustrations.

_____ **Functional Fossils** Make a model of a plant or animal fossil. Describe what the fossil might tell about the age of the rock it was found in. Explain how scientists use fossils to determine relative ages.

_____ **A Scientist's Story** Write a short story about a scientist who is researching the relative dates of sedimentary rocks in a town. The scientists should explain the law of superposition and talk about how that law helps date the rocks.

Side Dishes

_____ **Explaining Geologic Columns** Imagine you are a scientist at a conference. Present a speech in which you explain the idea behind geologic columns. In your speech, include information about how scientists collect information about geologic columns and how scientists use geologic columns.

_____ **Important Principles** Imagine you are working with scientists on a newly discovered island. Make a diagram or model of the island's geologic column. Explain the relative ages of rock layers.

Desserts (optional)

_____ **Understanding Unconformities** Design a poster about the different ways that layers can be changed or disturbed. Include labels and brief descriptions on your poster.

Absolute Dating

Alternative Assessment

Tic-Tac-Toe: *Create a Museum Exhibit*

Suppose you are an expert in absolute dating, and you have offered to help a local museum create an exhibit about Earth's age.

1. Work on your own, with a partner, or with a small group.

2. Choose three quick activities from the game. Check the boxes you plan to complete. They must form a straight line in any direction.

3. Have your teacher approve your plan.

4. Do each activity, and turn in your results.

__ **Half-Life Breakdown**	__ **You Ask the Questions**	__ **Which Is Best?**
Create a display for the museum exhibit that explains what half-life is. The poster should also discuss how scientists use half-life in radiometric dating.	The exhibit you're creating will have an interactive quiz for visitors to take. Write a quiz that contains at least four questions about index fossils and the ways scientists use them.	The museum's director wants a display showing radiometric dating of one rock sample. They have sedimentary, igneous, and metamorphic samples. Write a memo to the director, telling which sample to use and why.
__ **Decay Drama**	__ **Dating Description**	__ **Absolute Persuasion**
Develop and put on a skit to show visitors how radioactive decay makes it possible for scientists to date objects.	Create a multimedia presentation that lists and describes the different methods of radiometric dating. Include information about the best situations in which to use each method.	Museum donors are unsure whether they want to pay you to develop the exhibit. They do not understand what absolute dating is. Give a persuasive speech in which you explain what absolute dating is and why the exhibit is needed.
__ **Meeting the Requirements**	__ **Come on Down!**	__ **How Old Is Earth?**
Design a Web page that will help bring people to the new exhibit. On the page, discuss the requirements fossils must meet to be considered index fossils.	To encourage press coverage of the exhibit, you must write a press release. Write a press release that explains what absolute dating is and why people should visit the exhibit.	Create and perform a song that will play at the new museum exhibit. In your song, describe how scientists determine Earth's age.

The Geologic Time Scale

Choose Your Meal: *Earth's History*
Make a meal that shows what you know about Earth's geologic past.

1. Work on your own, with a partner, or with a small group.

2. Choose one item from each section of the menu, with an optional dessert. Check your choices.

3. Have your teacher approve your plan.

4. Submit or present your results.

Appetizers

_____ **Big Change Coming** Draw a picture of a geologic event that could cause a sudden change to Earth's surface.

_____ **Name Game** Research how geologists came up with the names of different periods in the geologic time scale. Share your results with the class in a presentation.

Main Dishes

_____ **Earth Diary** Write a diary entry for each era of the Phanerozoic eon. In your entries, describe climate conditions and at least one major geologic event.

_____ **Interview from the Past** Write a newspaper article about an interview with Scottish farmer and scientist James Hutton. Ask *how, what, why, where,* and *when* questions about geologic change over time.

Side Dishes

_____ **Lights Out** Design a model that shows how a major volcanic eruption would affect plants and other producers. Use simple materials in your model, such as a lamp, plants, and a piece of cloth.

_____ **On the Move** Plate tectonics results in the constant, slow movement of Earth's continents. Research the movement of the continents over Earth's history. Create a model of Earth's continents with moveable parts like a puzzle. Use it to demonstrate how the continents have moved at different times in Earth's history.

Dessert (optional)

_____ **Geologic Time Puzzle** Make a crossword puzzle that uses milestones in geologic time as clues for identifying Precambrian time and the eras of the Phanerozoic eon.

Tree Ring Analysis

Purpose This activity provides a means for assessing students' ability to use physical evidence to support the theory that climate change has taken place during Earth's past.

Time Period 30 minutes

Preparation You may wish to substitute a real tree ring in place of the diagram.

Teaching Strategies This activity can be assigned to individual students or to pairs of students.

Scoring Rubric

Possible points	Performance indicators
0–40	Quality and accuracy of labels made to tree ring diagram
0–60	Quality of answers to analysis questions

Tree Ring Analysis

Objective

You have learned that natural processes are responsible for changes the Earth has undergone throughout its long history. Rocks, fossils, and tree rings represent physical pieces of evidence for long term changes taking place during Earth's history. In this activity you will analyze an example tree ring to demonstrate how this type of analysis can be used to supply evidence for climate change.

Know the Score!

As you work through this activity, keep in mind that you will be earning a grade for the following:

- how well you label the tree ring diagram (40%)
- how well you answer the analysis questions (60%)

Procedure

1. When you saw through a tree to cut it down, you end up with a stump. The stump looks something like the example shown in the diagram below. The stump contains a series of rings that represent growth periods during the tree's life. Every year, a tree adds a new ring of cells to its trunk and those can be seen as distinct bands in the trunk cross section. External conditions can affect this growth. For example, more cells are added to the growing tree trunk when water availability is high. Fewer cells are added when water availability is low.

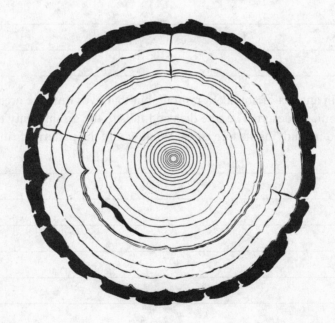

2. Study the diagram and label each of the following areas:

- the first year of the tree's life

- a year of higher than normal rainfall

- a two-year period of drought

- evidence of a forest fire

Analysis

3. Using this tree ring as an example, explain how tree ring analysis can be used as evidence for the theory that Earth's climate has changed in the past.

_____

_____

_____

_____

4. Both tree rings and fossil records are used to provide evidence of climate change on Earth. Which of these would you use to analyze recent climate changes and which would you use to analyze long ago changes? Explain your reasoning.

_____

_____

_____

_____

5. Suppose a tree grows in an area of abundant rainfall, but that over time the area becomes hotter and drier until it eventually becomes a desert. The tree dies and falls to the ground only to be picked up a year later by a scientist interested in studying its tree rings. What would the pattern of rings look like and why?

_____

_____

_____

_____

_____

Unit 2: Earth's History

Vocabulary

Fill in the blanks with the term that best completes the following sentences.

1. A _____ is the remains of a once-living organism found in layers of rock, ice, or amber.

2. The time required for half the quantity of a radioactive material to decay is its

   _____.

3. _____ is the theory stating that Earth's lithosphere is made up of large plates that

   are in constant motion.

4. _____ is the process in which a radioactive isotope tends to break down into a

   stable isotope.

5. _____ is the scientific study of the origin, physical history, and structure of Earth

   and the processes that shape it.

Key Concepts

Read each question below, and circle the best answer.

6. The diagram below shows a cross section of different rock layers. According to the law of superposition, the rock layer above another rock layer is younger than the one below.

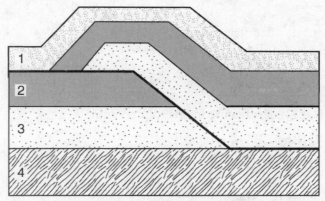

   According to the law of superposition, which numbered layer is the youngest?

   A. layer 1   C. layer 3

   B. layer 2   D. layer 4

7. Earth is approximately 4.6 billion years old. How do scientists determine this?

    A. by measuring the age of the oldest glaciers

    B. by using radiometric dating techniques on meteorites

    C. by measuring the age of the oldest fossils

    D. by determining the chemical composition of sea-floor sediments

8. Which best describes a fossil that was discovered in rock at the base of a cliff?

    A. it is likely younger than a fossil discovered in rock at the top of the cliff

    B. it is likely older than a fossil discovered in rock at the top of the cliff

    C. it is likely younger than a fossil discovered half way up the cliff

    D. it is most likely an index fossil

9. The law of crosscutting relationships states that a rock unit or geologic feature (such as a fault) is younger than any other rock unit it cuts through. A fault has shifted the rocks in the diagram below.

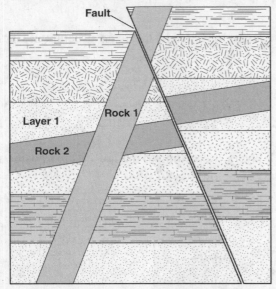

Fault

Rock 1

Layer 1

Rock 2

    Which of the following is the oldest feature in this rock column?

    A. Fault   C. Rock 2

    B. Rock 1   D. Layer 1

10. Which of these choices names two kinds of trace fossils?

    A. tracks and burrows   C. bee and beetle in amber

    B. shells and bones   D. petrified and mummified fossils

11. Earth's surface features slowly change over time. For example, sharp, jagged mountain ranges become lower and more rounded over time. What is responsible for this change in their shape?

    A. weathering and erosion   C. movement of continents

    B. deposition   D. collisions between continental plates

12. The figure below shows an arch, a geologic formation made over a long period of time by a process that supports the principle of uniformitarianism.

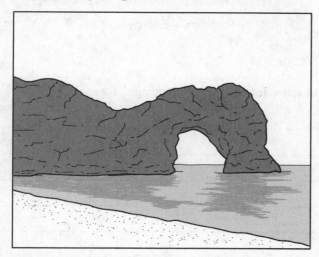

Which process below formed the arch shown in the figure?

A. precipitation   C. erosion

B. deposition   D. volcanism

13. Which statement best describes an index fossil?

A. a fossil that can be used to establish the absolute age of a rock layer

B. a fossil which is formed in soft sediment by the movement of an animal

C. a fossil of an insect captured in amber

D. a fossil of an animal captured in ice

Critical Thinking
Answer the following questions in the space provided.

14. List the four major divisions of Earth's history. Explain how these divisions were made and why they are useful.

_____

_____

_____

_____

_____

15. Scientists study how radioactive isotopes in rocks, such as Carbon-14, decay to tell the age of the rock.

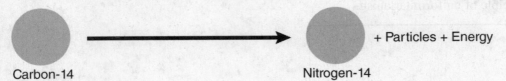

Carbon-14   Nitrogen-14   + Particles + Energy

Explain how knowing the half-life of Carbon 14 can tell scientists the absolute age of a rock sample.

_____

_____

_____

_____

_____

Connect ESSENTIAL QUESTIONS

Lessons 1 and 3

Answer the following question in the space provided.

16. Explain how fossils and other materials can tell us about the conditions of an area at the time it existed. Then explain how you could find the ages of these fossils and other materials.

_____

_____

_____

_____

_____

_____

Earth's History

Key Concepts
Choose the letter of the best answer.

1. Jacob has one older brother and one younger sister. He wants to explain relative dating to them using their ages as an example. Which of these statements describes their ages using relative dating?

   A. Their ages are 14, 12, and 9.

   B. They are all about the same age.

   C. The boys have different ages than the girl.

   D. Jacob is younger than his brother, but older than his sister.

2. The diagram below shows one kind of radioactive decay that is used for dating.

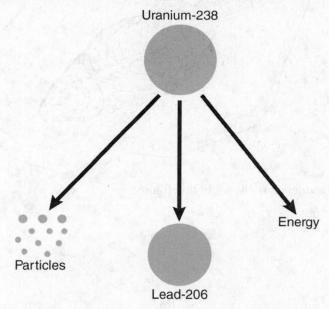

When a rock formed, it contained the parent isotope, uranium-238, but it did not contain the daughter isotope. How would this rock change over time?

   A. The amount of uranium-238 would increase, and the amount of lead-206 would decrease.

   B. The amount of uranium-238 would decrease, and the amount of lead-206 would increase.

   C. The amount of uranium-238 would stay the same, and the amount of lead-206 would increase.

   D. The amount of uranium-238 would decrease, and the amount of lead-206 would stay the same.

3. A team of geologists compared the rock layers found in Florida to those found in northwest Africa. They placed all of the rock layers from the two regions in order from youngest to oldest. What did the team make?

   A. a fossil record

   B. a geologic record

   C. a geologic column

   D. a topographic map

4. The figure below shows one type of physical evidence that scientists use to understand Earth's past.

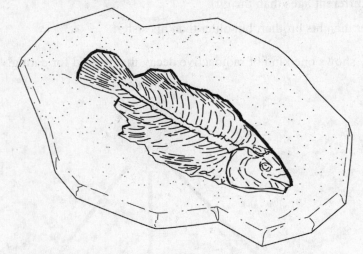

   What type of physical evidence is shown in this figure?

   A. fossil

   B. ice core

   C. coprolite

   D. tree rings

5. Which property of fossils allows scientists to determine the relative ages of rock layers?

   A. Fossils show change over time as species evolve.

   B. Fossils form from the remains of living organisms.

   C. Fossils are usually found only in sedimentary rock.

   D. Fossils can be analyzed to determine their exact ages.

6. In the 1830s, an English scientist proposed the idea of uniformitarianism to describe the process of geologic change on Earth. Which of the following words is most closely associated with uniformitarianism?

   A. rare

   B. sudden

   C. gradual

   D. catastrophic

7. The composition of sedimentary rock shows the source of the sediment that makes up the rock. Which of the following would provide the best evidence of how the rock formed?

   A. the rock's age

   B. the rock's color

   C. the rock's texture

   D. the rock's fossil content

8. The existence of humans on Earth represents a very short amount of time on the geologic time scale. In which epoch do we currently live?

   A. Eocene

   B. Pliocene

   C. Holocene

   D. Pleistocene

9. The table below shows some of the major events in Earth's history.

Time (Millions of years before present)	Event
0.01	end of last glacial period
2.6	early human ancestors appear
65.5	extinction of the dinosaurs
251	largest mass extinction event in Earth's history
542	first animals with exoskeletons appear
4,600	formation of Earth

Which event marks the end of Precambrian time?

A. formation of Earth

B. extinction of the dinosaurs

C. first animals with exoskeletons appear

D. largest mass extinction event in Earth's history

10. Sometimes a fossil is formed as a result of the movement of an organism in soft sediment. What type of fossil is this called?

    A. bone fossil

    B. trace fossil

    C. frozen fossil

    D. petrified fossil

11. Early in the history of geology, scientists debated two different views of how geologic processes work. These two ideas became known as uniformitarianism and catastrophism. Which of the following correctly describes the early view of catastrophism?

A. Geologic changes can either be sudden or gradual.

B. Geologic changes can quickly change Earth's structure.

C. Geologic changes only occur in sudden, devastating events.

D. Geologic changes only occur because of slow, gradual processes.

12. Basalt is a gray or black igneous rock. Pilar uses an absolute dating method to study a sample of basalt. Which of the following phrases represents the age of the rock in years?

A. half-life of the rock

B. absolute age of the rock

C. radiocarbon age of the rock

D. age of the index fossil in the rock

Critical Thinking

Answer the following questions in the space provided.

13. Scientists have determined the ages of rock samples from other places in the solar system. What is one type of extraterrestrial rock for which scientists have determined an absolute age? How do the ages of these rocks compare to the ages of the oldest rocks on Earth?

_____

_____

Extended Response

Answer the following questions in the space provided.

14. Look at this diagram of rock layers.

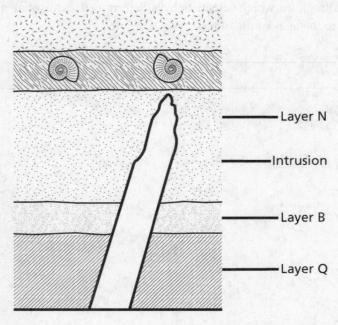

What is the relative age of the intrusion compared to layer B? Which law or principle did you use to arrive at your answer?

_____

_____

_____

In which order did the Layers B, N, and Q form? Which law or principle did you use to arrive at your answer?

_____

_____

_____

Earth's History

Key Concepts
Choose the letter of the best answer.

1. Jacob has one older brother and one younger sister. He wants to explain relative dating to them using their ages as an example. Which of the following arrangements would show the concept of relative dating?

   A. forming a line in the order of age

   B. forming a line in the order of height

   C. forming a line in the order of weight

   D. forming a line in the order of birth month

2. The diagram below shows one kind of radioactive decay that is used for dating.

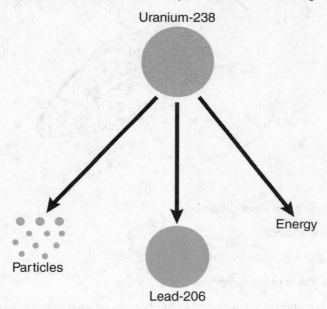

   Which statement best describes what information is needed to determine the age of a rock sample using this type of dating method?

   A. the exact mass of uranium-238 in the sample

   B. the amount of lead-206 present in the sample

   C. the energy being released by the uranium-238

   D. the relative amounts of uranium-238 and lead-206

3. A scientist wants to make a geologic column of rock layers from different parts of a state. How will the scientist do this?

   A. The scientists will look at the surface features in each area to organize the layers.

   B. The scientist will organize the layers by comparing the fossils and types of rocks.

   C. The scientist will measure the exact ages of the rocks found in each part of the state.

   D. The scientist will select one area in the state and use only those layers to construct the geologic column.

4. The figure below shows one type of physical evidence that scientists use to understand Earth's past. Imagine that you found this evidence on a mountaintop.

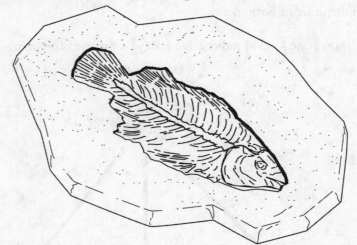

   What could you conclude from your discovery?

   A. This organism is now extinct.

   B. This fossil is older than the mountaintop.

   C. The mountaintop is made of metamorphic rock.

   D. The rocks on this mountaintop were once at the bottom of an ocean.

5. How do scientists use fossils to determine the relative ages of rock layers?

   A. by comparing all the fossils in one rock layer

   B. by comparing fossils in many different rock layers

   C. by determining the positions of fossils in many different rock layers

   D. by locating other areas of the world where the same fossils are found

6. In the 1830s, an English scientist proposed the idea of uniformitarianism to describe the process of geologic change on Earth. Which of the following is most accurately described by uniformitarianism?

   A. erosion

   B. extinction

   C. an earthquake

   D. a volcanic eruption

7. The composition of sedimentary rock shows the source of the sediment that makes up the rock. Which of the following is a type of sedimentary rock that forms from once-living plants and animals?

   A. quartz

   B. calcite

   C. limestone

   D. sandstone

8. The existence of humans on Earth represents a very short amount of time on the geologic time scale. Which of the following is the period in which we currently live?

   A. Tertiary

   B. Holocene

   C. Cenozoic

   D. Quaternary

9. The table below shows some of the major events in Earth's history.

Time (Millions of years before present)	Event
0.01	end of last glacial period
2.6	early human ancestors appear
65.5	extinction of the dinosaurs
251	largest mass extinction event in Earth's history
542	first animals with exoskeletons appear
4,600	formation of Earth

   Which event marks the end of the Permian Period?

   A. extinction of the dinosaurs

   B. early human ancestors appear

   C. first animals with exoskeletons appear

   D. largest mass extinction event in Earth's history

10. Sometimes a fossil is formed as a result of the movement of an organism in soft sediment. Which of the following are two kinds of trace fossils?

    A. shells and bones

    B. tracks and burrows

    C. bee and beetle in amber

    D. petrified and mummified fossils

11. Early in the history of geology, scientists debated two different views of how geologic processes work. These two ideas became known as uniformitarianism and catastrophism. Which of the following is an example of the modern view of uniformitarianism and catastrophism?

A. Earth's surface is reshaped only through slow, gradual geologic processes.

B. Some geologic processes happen quickly, while others happen over millions of years.

C. Geologic changes that reshape Earth's surface only occur in sudden, devastating events.

D. Early in Earth's history, geologic change was mostly catastrophic but is now mostly uniform.

12. Basalt is a gray or black igneous rock. Pilar uses an absolute dating method to study a sample of basalt. What will the method help her learn about the basalt sample?

A. the age of the sample

B. the physical structure of the sample

C. the mineral composition of the sample

D. the geographic distribution of the sample

Critical Thinking
Answer the following questions in the space provided.

13. Scientists have determined the ages of rock samples from other places in the solar system. Why are rock samples from other parts of the solar system useful for determining the age of Earth?

_____

_____

Extended Response
Answer the following questions in the space provided.

14. Look at this diagram of rock layers.

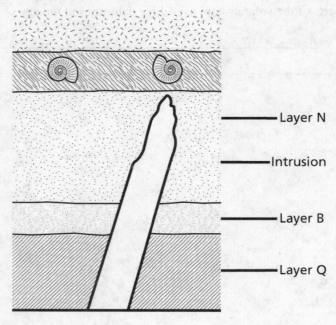

Layer N
Intrusion
Layer B
Layer Q

What is the relative age of the intrusion compared to layer Q? Explain your answer, including what law or principle you used to arrive at your answer.

_____

_____

_____

In which order did the labeled rock formations form? Explain your answer, including any laws or principles you used to arrive at your answer.

_____

_____

_____

Minerals and Rocks

Choose the letter of the best answer.

1. The diagram below shows a cross section of a volcano during an eruption.

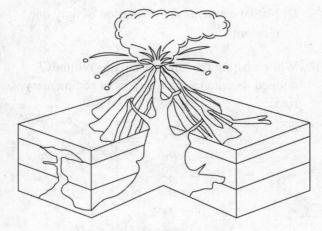

Which term describes the rock that will eventually form on the surface as a result of the eruption?

A. foliated

B. intrusive

C. extrusive

D. nonfoliated

2. Over time, repeated cycles of heating and cooling can cause a rock to crack. The rock may then break into smaller pieces. What is this process called?

A. erosion

B. deposition

C. subsidence

D. weathering

3. Metamorphic rocks are classified according to their texture. Which of the following describes nonfoliated texture?

A. mineral grains that all have similar sizes

B. mineral grains arranged in planes or bands

C. mineral grains arranged in random positions

D. mineral grains that have a range of different sizes

4. The table below shows the Mohs hardness scale.

Hardness	Mineral
1	talc
2	gypsum
3	calcite
4	fluorite
5	apatite
6	feldspar
7	quartz
8	topaz
9	corundum
10	diamond

A scientist rubs an unknown mineral against samples of calcite and apatite. The mineral leaves a scratch on both samples. Which of the following is the unknown mineral?

A. apatite

B. calcite

C. fluorite

D. gypsum

5. A volcanic eruption took place about 2 billion years ago and released lava onto Earth's surface. The lava cooled to form basalt. Which of the following is least likely to have happened to the basalt over this time?

   A. Some of the basalt changed into metamorphic rock.

   B. Some of the basalt melted and became molten rock.

   C. Most of the basalt stayed the same for 2 billion years.

   D. Most of the basalt broke down and became sediment.

6. Mountain ranges can be produced when tectonic plates collide and push areas of Earth's crust to higher elevations. What is the correct term for this process?

   A. uplift

   B. erosion

   C. deposition

   D. subsidence

7. Sedimentary rocks can form in several different ways. Which of the following are all different types of sedimentary rock?

   A. chemical, clastic, organic

   B. clastic, inorganic, chemical

   C. organic, clastic, nonfoliated

   D. crystalline, chemical, organic

8. Lamont has a dark container. He knows that the container has a mass of 2.0 g when it is empty. He cannot see inside the container. However, he is able to use a balance to determine that the container has a mass of 2.7 g. What can Lamont conclude about the container?

   A. It contains matter.

   B. It contains a solid.

   C. It contains energy.

   D. It contains a liquid.

9. What makes native elements different from other nonsilicate minerals?

   A. Native elements contain sulfur compounds.

   B. Native elements contain silicon compounds.

   C. Native elements contain oxygen compounds.

   D. Native elements are composed of only one element.

10. While visiting the Grand Canyon, Whitney noticed it contains many layers of sedimentary rock.

How did the sedimentary rock most likely form?

   A. by magma slowly cooling and changing into solid rock

   B. by heat and pressure creating separate layers of materials

   C. by lava from volcanic eruptions cooling on Earth's surface

   D. by sand and other materials being deposited and hardening over time

Minerals

Choose the letter of the best answer.

1. Which properties describe all matter?

   A. having volume and charge

   B. having mass and taking up space

   C. having atoms and taking up space

   D. having molecules and temperature

2. Which of these is a silicate mineral?

   A. gold

   B. mica

   C. halite

   D. oxygen

3. Diamond is a valuable mineral that is made up of carbon atoms arranged in a repeating pattern. This repeating pattern gives diamonds their hardness. Which of these characteristics do diamonds share with all minerals?

   A. extreme hardness

   B. rarity and high cost

   C. orderly crystal structure

   D. made up of carbon atoms

4. Stalactites and stalagmites are two cone-shaped mineral formations that form in caves. Stalactites hang down from the ceiling, and stalagmites rise up from the cave floor. What causes cave minerals to form in this way?

   A. Molten rock cools and hardens as it reaches Earth's surface.

   B. Groundwater heated by molten rock reacts with minerals in the rock to form new minerals.

   C. Existing minerals change into new minerals when nearby molten rock causes an increase in temperature.

   D. Groundwater carrying dissolved materials combines with surface water and causes minerals to precipitate out of solution.

5. The drawing below shows the cleavage of four minerals.

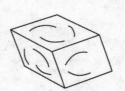
Calcite

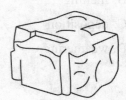
Halite

Fluorite

Muscovite

A scientist studies a sample of an unknown mineral. She notices that it can form perfect cubes when it breaks. What kind of mineral could this be?

   A. calcite

   B. fluorite

   C. halite

   D. muscovite

The Rock Cycle

Choose the letter of the best answer.

1. When a volcano erupts, ash can enter Earth's atmosphere. Eventually, the ash falls back down to Earth's surface. Which term describes the falling of volcanic ash to Earth's surface?

    A. erosion

    B. deposition

    C. subsidence

    D. weathering

2. The flow chart below shows how a metamorphic rock can change into a sedimentary rock.

    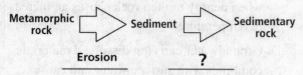

    Which term should replace the question mark?

    A. cooling

    B. melting

    C. deposition

    D. weathering

3. A large amount of sediment is deposited on a plain in a short amount of geologic time. Which of the following correctly describes a possible result?

    A. The crust is uplifted due to groundwater infiltrating the sediment.

    B. The crust subsides due to the weight of the sediment that accumulates.

    C. The crust subsides due to the motion of the sediment as it is deposited.

    D. The crust is uplifted due to the difference in weight between the sediment and bedrock.

4. Which of these phrases defines *subsidence*?

    A. Earth's crust rising

    B. Earth's crust sinking

    C. Earth's crust shifting sideways

    D. Earth's crust moving in any direction

5. Declan observed a rock that he found at the beach. The rock felt hard, it was yellow, and it appeared to be made of layers. Declan concluded that the rock was sedimentary. Which observation best supports this conclusion?

    A. the yellow color

    B. the hardness of the rock

    C. the layers within the rock

    D. the location where the rock was found

Three Classes of Rock

Choose the letter of the best answer.

1. The diagram below shows a river forming a delta as it slows down and enters the sea. As the river slows down, it deposits large amounts of sediment.

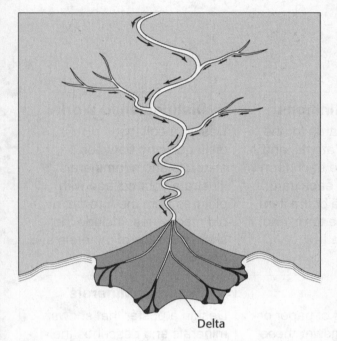

Delta

Which term describes the rock that will eventually form from the sediment?

A. clastic

B. organic

C. foliated

D. extrusive

2. Which of the following is a direct source of material for the formation of metamorphic rock?

A. clasts

B. magma

C. sediments

D. existing rock

3. Granite forms when liquid magma slowly cools within Earth's crust. If the granite is exposed to intense heat and pressure, it can change to gneiss. Which type of change takes place when granite turns into gneiss?

A. Sedimentary rock changes to igneous rock.

B. Igneous rock changes to metamorphic rock.

C. Metamorphic rock changes to igneous rock.

D. Sedimentary rock changes to metamorphic rock.

4. Igneous rocks form when magma cools and solidifies. As the magma cools, minerals form. What effect will the rate at which the magma cools have on the texture of the igneous rock?

A. the faster the magma cools, the smaller the crystals in the rock will be

B. the slower the magma cools, the smaller the crystals in the rock will be

C. the faster the magma cools, the more foliated the rock's texture will be

D. the slower the magma cools, the more foliated the rock's texture will be

5. Which of the following correctly describes the difference between a mineral and a rock?

A. Rock can be made of inorganic material, but minerals are always organic.

B. Rocks are made of naturally occurring material, but minerals can be synthetic.

C. Rocks are made of crystalline material, but minerals are always noncrystalline.

D. Rock can be made of noncrystalline material, but minerals are always crystals.

Minerals

Tic-Tac-Toe: *Matter and Minerals*
Complete the activities to show what you've learned about matter and minerals.

1. Work on your own, with a partner, or with a small group.

2. Choose three quick activities from the game. Check the boxes you plan to complete. They must form a straight line in any direction.

3. Have your teacher approve your plan.

4. Do each activity, and turn in your results.

__ **You Ask the Questions**	__ **Trading Definitions**	__ **Distinguished Work**
Compose a quiz that contains at least six questions. Write about the ways minerals form. Include different types of questions such as multiple choice, true/false, and short answer.	Design trading cards for the terms *elements*, *atoms*, and *compounds*. Give each term its own card. On each card, draw an example of the item, label it, define the term, and, if appropriate, list a few examples.	Design a collage distinguishing between minerals and nonminerals. Illustrate your collage with pictures from the Internet or old magazines. Include the characteristics of minerals and nonminerals.
__ **Presenting Properties**	__ **You Decide**	__ **Picturing Minerals**
Make a PowerPoint presentation in which you compare and contrast properties of common minerals. Include illustrations or diagrams.	On a small sheet of paper or an index card, answer these questions: *What did you know about minerals before reviewing this lesson? What did you learn about minerals that you did not know before?*	Design a poster that shows minerals and describes their characteristics. Include illustrations or pictures of common minerals. Also list characteristics that all minerals share.
__ **Pair Match Up**	__ **What Am I?**	__ **Guess the Mineral**
Make cards about minerals' physical properties (for example, *color*, *streak*, *luster*, *hardness*, *density*, *cleavage*, and *fracture*). Then make another card that will pair with each property (for example, word definitions, an illustration, and so on). Play a matching game. See who can match the most pairs.	Present a skit in which two actors are different minerals who compare their properties. For example, one actor might be a silicate mineral and another actor a nonsilicate mineral. The actors can talk about their properties and the things that make them different from each other. Then have the class guess who is the silicate mineral and who is the nonsilicate mineral.	Design a game that shows you know the ways to identify minerals. On index cards, write the name of some minerals and how to identify them. To play, draw a card and describe how to identify the mineral. Other players try to guess the mineral.

Unit 3 Lesson 2

Alternative Assessment

The Rock Cycle

Mix and Match: *Changes to Rock Types*

Mix and match ideas to show what you've learned about the rock cycle and the ways rock types change.

1. Work on your own, with a partner, or with a small group.

2. Choose one information source from Column A, two topics from Column B, and one option from Column C. Check your choices.

3. Have your teacher approve your plan.

4. Submit or present your results.

A. Choose Two Rock Types and Processes	B. Choose Two Things to Analyze	C. Choose One Way to Communicate Analysis
____ igneous rock	____ observable properties and characteristics	____ news report or news article
____ sedimentary rock	____ details	____ fictional story or monologue
____ metamorphic rock	____ causes or formation	____ poster or illustration
____ weathering	____ types and variations	____ game
____ erosion		____ questionnaire or worksheet
____ deposition		____ invented dialogue or interview
		____ model or diorama
		____ commercial or video
		____ PowerPoint presentation
		____ a skit or performance

Three Classes of Rock

Take Your Pick: *It Rocks!*
Complete the activities to show what you've learned about the three classes of rock.

1. Work on your own, with a partner, or with a small group.

2. Choose items below for a minimum total of 10 points. Check your choices.

3. Have your teacher approve your plan.

4. Submit or present your results.

2 Points

_____ **Rock and Roll** Create an original song that explains how rock is classified and describes the three classes of rock. Record your song, and play it or sing it for the class.

_____ **Rockin' Art** Design a poster or other art project that shows the three classes of rock and how each forms. Include details and examples of each type of rock.

5 Points

_____ **Pet Rock** Find a rock of any type. Decorate your new pet to personalize it, but leave some of the original rock surface visible. Figure out whether your rock is igneous, sedimentary, or metamorphic. Write a short paper explaining what type of rock it is and how you know.

_____ **Rock Models** Create a model for each class of rock: sedimentary, igneous, and metamorphic. Label each model, and include a place of origin and a story about how it formed.

_____ **Take a Hike** Go on a rock hunt. Gather at least 10 varied rock samples. Afterwards, classify them as to type. Place each rock in a plastic bag. Attach labels, and tell how you made identifications.

_____ **Floating Rock** Pumice is an extrusive igneous rock that has a surprising characteristic… it floats! Research this rock type. Write a report or draw a diagram detailing how pumice forms and why it floats. If possible, find a sample of pumice to share with the class.

8 Points

_____ **Rock Puzzle** Design a crossword puzzle about rocks. First, make a list of a minimum of 15 terms you want to use. Next, put these words into puzzle format. Finally, write clues that give details and information about each term. Test your puzzle on classmates or your teacher.

_____ **Movie Rocks** Write a script describing how each of the three rock types and their subtypes (intrusive and extrusive igneous; clastic, chemical, and organic sedimentary; and foliated and nonfoliated metamorphic) are formed. Film your movie, and share it with your class.

Minerals

Purpose In this activity, students will use the physical properties of minerals and other characteristics to identify minerals.

Time Period 45–60 minutes

Preparation Gather 5 different mineral samples and label them *A, B, C, D,* and *E.* Make note of which mineral each sample is. Mineral samples can be purchased through a scientific supply house. Mix a solution of 10% hydrochloric acid and pour into dropper bottles. Equip each station with the necessary materials prior to starting the activity. Have paper towels on hand to clean up any water spills.

Safety Tips Have students review all safety icons before beginning the activity. Point out water sources for students to use if they spill the hydrochloric acid. Although the acid is diluted, caution should still be used. If students do spill acid, make sure to flush the area well with water. Spilled water is a slippage hazard and should be wiped up immediately. Have students handle the minerals and glass carefully and wash their hands thoroughly when they are done testing the minerals with their fingernails.

Teaching Strategies This activity works best in pairs. Students will be observing the characteristics used to classify minerals in this activity, so review with students properties used by scientists to classify minerals. List the Mohs scale for the following items on the board: fingernail (Mohs 2), penny (Mohs 3), glass (Mohs 5.5), steel file (Mohs 6.5), sandpaper (9).

Scoring Rubric

Possible points	Performance indicators
0–20	Lab technique
0–40	Quality and clarity of observations
0–40	Identification of minerals and explanation of observations

Minerals

Objective

Scientists use observations about the physical characteristics and properties of minerals to identify and classify minerals. In this activity, you will observe the characteristics and properties of minerals.

Know the Score!

As you work through this activity, keep in mind that you will be earning a grade for the following:

- how well you work with materials and equipment (20%)

- how well you record your observations and graph data (40%)

- how well you explain those observations, including correct identification of minerals (40%)

Materials and Equipment

- dilute hydrochloric acid, in dropper bottle
- glass
- gloves
- hand lens
- lab apron
- magnet
- mineral samples

- penny
- petri dish
- safety goggles
- sandpaper
- steel file
- streak plate

Safety Information

- Locate water sources. If an acid spill occurs, flush the area well with water and notify your teacher immediately.

- Spilled water is a slipping hazard. Clean any spills immediately.

- Handle glass carefully.

- Wash hands thoroughly after handling minerals.

Procedure

1. Observe each of the five mineral samples. Record your observations about the minerals' color and luster in the data table. Use words such as metallic, nonmetallic, glassy, and pearly to describe luster.

Properties of Minerals

Sample	Color	Luster	Hardness	Streak	Magnetism	Acid Test
A						
B						
C						
D						
E						

2. Use the Mohs scale to determine hardness. Use the following materials to scratch each sample: your fingernail, a penny, a piece of glass, a steel file, and sandpaper. Use the results and the Mohs scale data your teacher provides to determine the hardness of each sample and record the information in the table.

3. Rub each mineral across the streak glass. Record observations about each mineral's streak in the table.

4. Place Sample A in a petri dish. Drop a few drops of dilute hydrochloric acid on the sample and observe what happens. Record your observations in the table. Then repeat for the remaining samples.

Analysis

5. Using information from the table and a mineral guide, identify the samples.

   Sample A: _____

   Sample B: _____

   Sample C: _____

   Sample D: _____

   Sample E: _____

6. Which physical properties of the minerals did you not test? How could you test for them?

   _____

7. Would you have been able to identify the minerals if you only tested for one or two characteristics? Explain.

   _____

   _____

Unit 3: Minerals and Rocks

Vocabulary

Fill in each blank with the term that best completes the following sentences.

1. The _____ is a series of geologic processes in which rock can form, change from one type to another, be destroyed, and form again.

2. Changes in temperature or pressure, or chemical processes, can transform an existing rock into a

    _____ rock.

3. A _____ is a naturally occurring, solid combination of one or more minerals or

    organic matter.

4. The rising of regions of Earth's crust to higher elevations is called _____.

5. _____ is a physical property used to describe how the surface of a mineral reflects

    light.

Key Concepts

Read each question below, and circle the best answer.

6. The table below lists five classes of nonsilicate minerals.

Class	Description	Example
Carbonates	contain carbon and oxygen compounds	calcite
Halides	contain ions of chlorine, fluorine, iodine, and bromine	halite
Native elements	contain only one type of atom	gold
Oxides	contain oxygen compounds	hematite
Sulfides	contain sulfur compounds	pyrite

There are actually six classes of nonsilicate minerals. Which class is missing from this chart?

A. feldspars   C. silicates

B. micas   D. sulfates

7. Granite can form when magma cools within Earth. Basalt can form when lava cools on Earth's surface. What do granite and basalt have in common?

A. They are igneous.

B. They are old.

C. They are fossils.

D. They are intrusive

8. A student is testing a mineral in science class.

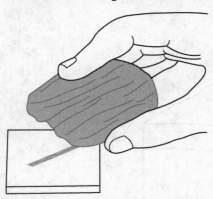

What property of the mineral is the student testing?

A. cleavage   C. luster

B. color   D. streak

9. Which one of the following statements about elements, atoms, and compounds is not true?

A. Elements consist of one type of atom and can combine to form compounds.

B. Compounds are smaller than atoms.

C. Elements and compounds form the basis of all materials on Earth.

D. Atoms cannot be broken down into smaller substances.

10. Which of the following best describes how sedimentary rock forms?

A. molten rock beneath the surface of Earth cools and becomes solid

B. layers of sediment become compressed over time to form rock

C. chemical processes or changes in pressure or temperature change a rock

D. molten rock reaches the surface and cools to become solid rock

11. Study the diagram below.

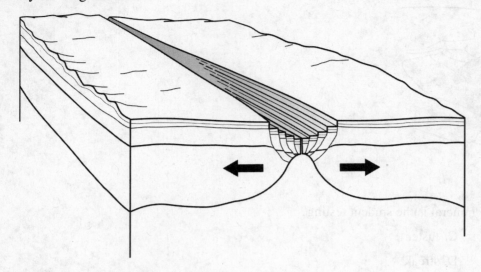

What process is occurring in this image?

A. two tectonic plates are moving toward each other, creating a syncline

B. two tectonic plates are pulling away from each other, creating a rift zone

C. two tectonic plates are moving toward each other, creating an anticline

D. two tectonic plates are moving away from each other, creating a new mountain range.

12. Over time, repeated temperature changes can cause a rock to break down into smaller pieces. What is this an example of?

A. subsidence   C. deposition

B. weathering   D. erosion

Critical Thinking
Answer the following questions in the space provided.

13. You are standing by a cliff far away from the ocean. You see a sedimentary layer with shells in it. You are told the shells are from oceanic organisms. How do you think this layer formed?

_____

_____

_____

_____

14. The diagram below shows the rock cycle.

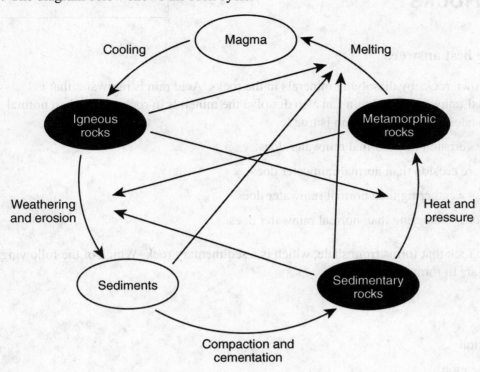

The rock cycle describes how rocks change. What conditions must be present for igneous or sedimentary rock to change into metamorphic rock? Name two ways that this could happen.

_____

_____

_____

Connect ESSENTIAL QUESTIONS

Lessons 2 and 3

Answer the following question in the space provided.

15. Explain a way that a sedimentary rock could form, then over time break down into smaller pieces, and become a sedimentary rock again in another location.

_____

_____

_____

_____

_____

Minerals and Rocks

Key Concepts
Choose the letter of the best answer.

1. Rainwater can break down rocks by dissolving minerals in the rocks. Acid rain is rainwater that is more acidic than normal rainwater. Acid rain can also dissolve the minerals in rocks faster than normal rainwater can. Which statement about acid rain is true?

   A. Acid rain causes less erosion than normal rainwater does.

   B. Acid rain causes more erosion than normal rainwater does.

   C. Acid rain causes less weathering than normal rainwater does.

   D. Acid rain causes more weathering than normal rainwater does.

2. Slate is a metamorphic rock that forms from shale, which is a sedimentary rock. Which of the following would be needed for slate to form from shale?

   A. weathering

   B. heat and pressure

   C. erosion and deposition

   D. melting and solidification

3. The diagram shown below shows a rift zone forming between two oceanic plates.

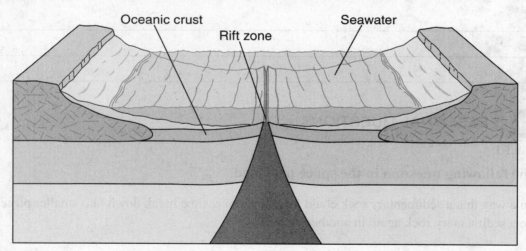

   Which of these actions is shown just below the center of the rift zone?

   A. subduction

   B. magma flowing up

   C. lava becoming solid

   D. continental crust melting

4. Rocks of all types can be classified according to their texture. Which of the following correctly describes texture?

A. It describes the sizes, shapes, and colors of the grains that make up the rock.

B. It describes the sizes, shapes, and densities of the grains that make up the rock.

C. It describes the sizes, shapes, and positions of the grains that make up the rock.

D. It describes the sizes, shapes, and compositions of the grains that make up the rock

5. Minerals make up most of the rocks on Earth's surface. What are three changes that can cause minerals to form by metamorphism?

A. pressure, temperature, melting

B. pressure, physical makeup, melting

C. temperature, melting, physical makeup

D. temperature, pressure, chemical makeup

6. Which change of state takes place when magma turns into igneous rock?

A. gas to solid

B. solid to gas

C. solid to liquid

D. liquid to solid

7. The table below lists the masses and volumes of four mineral samples.

Mineral	Mass (g)	Volume (mL)
Feldspar	16	6.2
Galena	9	1.2
Garnet	12	3.0
Quartz	10	3.7

Which mineral has the greatest density?

A. feldspar

B. galena

C. garnet

D. quartz

8. These diagrams show the arrangement of silicon and oxygen atoms in two different materials.

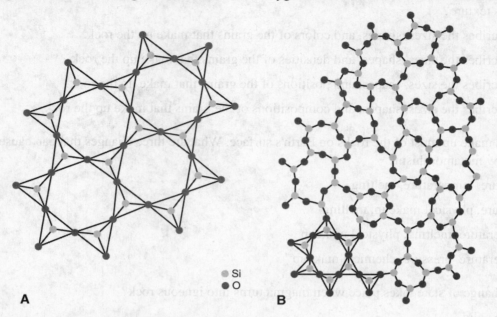

● Si
● O

A   B

Which statement **best** classifies these two materials and why?

A. They are both minerals because they contain silicon and oxygen atoms.

B. Only A is a mineral because it has an orderly arrangement and B does not.

C. Neither is a mineral because they both contain more than one type of atom.

D. Only B is a mineral because it has rings with more than six atoms and A does not.

9. Basalt is a dark-colored, fine-grained rock, and granite is a light-colored, coarse-grained rock. Which of the following correctly explains how each forms?

A. Basalt forms when lava cools, and granite forms when magma cools.

B. Basalt forms when magma cools, and granite forms when lava cools.

C. Basalt forms when lava cools, and granite forms when clasts are cemented.

D. Basalt forms when clasts are cemented, and granite forms when magma cools.

10. Conglomerate, sandstone, and siltstone are all examples of sedimentary rocks. Which of the following is the process of formation that these rocks have in common?

A. evaporation

B. cementation

C. solidification

D. condensation

11. The diagram below shows a large region of Earth's crust.

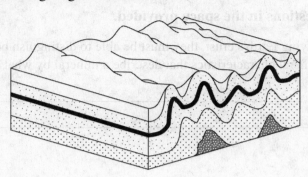

Which type of rock is forming deep below the surface?

A. intrusive igneous rock

B. extrusive igneous rock

C. foliated metamorphic rock

D. chemical sedimentary rock

12. Rocks are always a part of the rock cycle, even though they may stay in one part of it for millions of years. Which part of the rock cycle helps form igneous rock, but not other types of rock?

A. erosion

B. melting

C. deposition

D. metamorphism

Critical Thinking
Answer the following questions in the space provided.

13. When geologists are studying Earth's crust, they must be able to distinguish between minerals and nonminerals. List two mineral characteristics that describe a mineral by what it is made of.

   _____

   _____

Extended Response
Answer the following questions in the space provided.

14. All chemicals can be classified as elements or compounds. Describe how elements and compounds are related.

_____

_____

Name a mineral or type of mineral that is an example of each.

_____

_____

Minerals and Rocks

Key Concepts
Choose the letter of the best answer.

1. Rainwater can break down rocks by dissolving minerals in the rocks. Acid rain is rainwater that is more acidic than normal rainwater. Acid rain can also dissolve the minerals in rocks faster than normal rainwater can. How does acid rain affect different types of rock?

   A. It causes an equal amount of weathering in all types of rock.

   B. It changes sedimentary and igneous rocks into metamorphic rocks.

   C. It dissolves some rocks faster because of their different compositions.

   D. It causes metamorphic and sedimentary rocks to melt and form igneous rocks.

2. Slate is a metamorphic rock that forms from shale, which is a sedimentary rock. Which of the following would be needed for shale to form from slate?

   A. increased heat

   B. increased pressure

   C. erosion and deposition

   D. melting and solidification

3. The diagram shown below shows a rift zone forming between two oceanic plates.

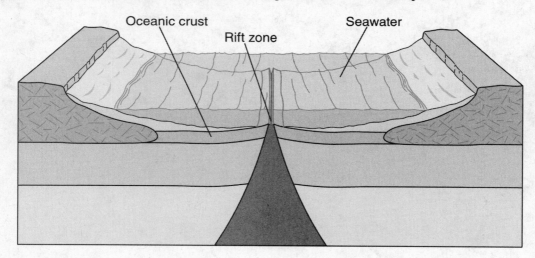

Oceanic crust   Rift zone   Seawater

   Which of the following correctly describes how the two tectonic plates are moving?

   A. One plate is sinking under the other.

   B. They are moving toward each other.

   C. They are moving away from each other.

   D. One plate is falling and the other is rising.

4. Rocks of all types can be classified according to their texture. Which of the following is an example of a rock texture?

    A. organic

    B. foliated

    C. intrusive

    D. light-colored

5. Minerals make up most of the rocks on Earth's surface. What is the difference between minerals that form from magma and those that form by metamorphism?

    A. Minerals that form from magma change their composition.

    B. Minerals that form from magma change from liquid to solid.

    C. Minerals that form from magma are altered by intense pressure.

    D. Minerals that form from magma are hotter than metamorphosed minerals.

6. Which physical change takes place when an igneous rock turns into sedimentary rock?

    A. weathering

    B. deformation

    C. pressure increases

    D. temperature decreases

7. The table below lists the densities of four different mineral samples.

Mineral	Density (g/mL)
Feldspar	2.6
Galena	7.5
Garnet	4.0
Quartz	2.7

    A sample of an unknown mineral has a mass of 32 g and a volume of 8.0 mL. Based on the information given in the table, which mineral is it?

    A. feldspar

    B. galena

    C. garnet

    D. quartz

8. These diagrams show the arrangement of silicon and oxygen atoms in two different materials.

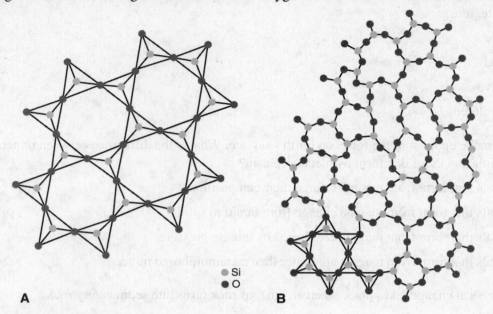

Si
O

A   B

What makes the material in diagram A a silicate mineral?

A. It contains oxygen atoms and atoms of at least one other element.

B. It is made up of an orderly arrangement of silicon and oxygen atoms.

C. It is made up of an orderly arrangement of more than one type of atom.

D. It is made up of silicon and oxygen atoms that have no particular pattern.

9. Basalt is a dark-colored, fine-grained rock, and granite is a light-colored, coarse-grained rock. Which term correctly identifies the class of rock that each rock belongs to?

A. Basalt is organic and granite is clastic.

B. Basalt is clastic and granite is organic.

C. Basalt is extrusive and granite is intrusive.

D. Basalt is intrusive and granite is extrusive.

10. Conglomerate, sandstone, and siltstone are all examples of sedimentary rocks. What do each of these rocks have in common?

A. They are all clastic sedimentary rocks.

B. They are all organic sedimentary rocks.

C. They are all foliated sedimentary rocks.

D. They are all chemical sedimentary rocks.

11. The diagram below shows a large region of Earth's crust.

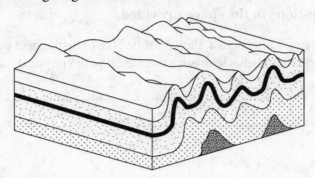

Which type of condition is changing the rock deep below the surface?

A. erosion

B. melting

C. weathering

D. high pressure

12. Rocks are always a part of the rock cycle, even though they may stay in one part of it for millions of years. Which part of the rock cycle helps form sedimentary rock, but not other types of rock?

A. erosion

B. melting

C. subduction

D. metamorphism

Critical Thinking
Answer the following questions in the space provided.

13. When geologists are studying Earth's crust, they must be able to distinguish between minerals and nonminerals. List two mineral characteristics that describe the physical nature of a mineral.

_____

_____

Extended Response
Answer the following questions in the space provided.

14. All chemicals can be classified as elements or compounds. Describe how elements and compounds
    are different.

    _____

    _____

    Classify quartz, gold, and diamond as either elements or compounds.

    _____

    _____

    _____

The Restless Earth

Choose the letter of the best answer.

1. The diagram below shows how seismic waves travel away from the place where an earthquake begins.

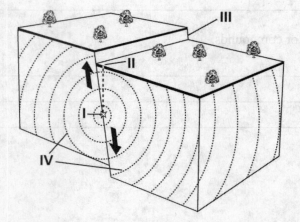

Which of the following correctly identifies the parts of the diagram?

A. I. Epicenter
   II. Focus
   III. Fault
   IV. Seismic wave

B. I. Epicenter
   II. Focus
   III. Seismic wave
   IV. Fault

C. I. Focus
   II. Epicenter
   III. Fault
   IV. Seismic wave

D. I. Focus
   II. Epicenter
   III. Seismic wave
   IV. Fault

2. Imagine you could travel in a straight line through Earth from a point on one side and come out on the other side. What compositional layer would you travel through in the exact center of Earth?

A. core
B. crust
C. lithosphere
D. mesosphere

3. Alternating quiet and violent eruptions are associated with which kind of volcano?

A. shield
B. composite
C. pyroclastic
D. cinder cone

4. Molten material flows gently out of a fissure on Earth's surface, then cools and hardens. This process happens again and again over geologic time. Eventually, what will form on the surface?

A. caldera
B. plate boundary
C. magma chamber
D. volcanic mountain

5. Tectonic plates can move toward each other and squeeze large blocks of rocks together, creating folded mountains. Which of the following terms describes a kind of fold in which the oldest rock layers are in the center of the fold?

A. syncline
B. anticline
C. symmetrical fold
D. asymmetrical fold

6. Notice how the figure below shows both continental crust and oceanic crust. In this figure, shading indicates density. The more darkly shaded a region is, the denser that region is.

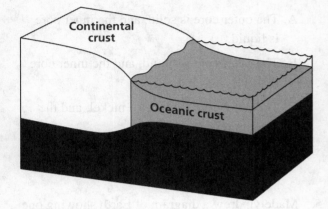

What can you infer from the figure?

A. Oceanic crust is denser than continental crust.

B. Continental crust is denser than oceanic crust.

C. Oceanic crust does not contain as much iron as continental crust.

D. Continental crust contains more magnesium than oceanic crust.

7. Convection currents in the mantle contribute to tectonic plate movement. What is a convection current?

A. the transfer of energy by direct contact

B. the transfer of energy by the movement of matter

C. the transfer of energy through a solid, such as the Earth's crust

D. the transfer of energy from a region of lower temperature to a region of higher temperature

8. What is the primary way that folded mountains are formed?

A. by tension

B. by shear stress

C. by compression

D. by volcanic activity

9. The diagram below shows Earth divided into five layers.

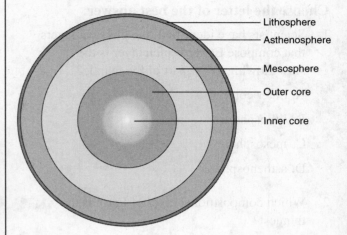

Scientists divide Earth into these layers based on what properties?

A. core properties

B. physical properties

C. chemical properties

D. atmospheric properties

10. What happens at a convergent tectonic plate boundary?

A. One tectonic plate pulls apart into two new plates, forming a rift or ridge.

B. Two tectonic plates pull away from one another, decreasing rock deformation.

C. Two tectonic plates collide with one another, causing subduction and/or mountain building.

D. Two tectonic plates slide horizontally past each other along Earth's surface, forming long fault lines.

Earth's Layers

Choose the letter of the best answer.

1. Scientists have identified five physical layers that compose Earth. Which layer is the slow-flowing lower part of the mantle?

   A. outer core

   B. lithosphere

   C. mesosphere

   D. asthenosphere

2. Which compositional layer of Earth is the thinnest?

   A. the crust

   B. the mantle

   C. the inner core

   D. the outer core

3. Evelyn is making a model of Earth to show how the physical layers correspond to the compositional layers. Which of the following should Evelyn show in her model?

   A. The physical layers exactly match the compositional layers.

   B. The crust is the only compositional layer not included in the physical layers.

   C. The physical layer of the asthenosphere includes the compositional layer of the crust.

   D. The physical layers of the inner core and outer core form a single compositional layer.

4. How is the outer core of Earth different from the inner core?

   A. The outer core is solid, and the inner core is liquid.

   B. The outer core is liquid, and the inner core is solid.

   C. The outer core is made of nickel, and the inner core is made of iron.

   D. The outer core is made of iron, and the inner core is made of nickel.

5. Madelyn drew a diagram of Earth showing one way that scientists have divided it. She included the core, the mantle, and the crust.

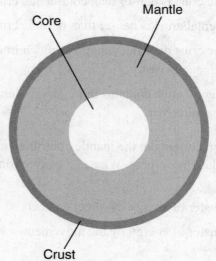

Madelyn divided her diagram into three layers based on which of the following?

   A. relative density

   B. physical structure

   C. geographical location

   D. chemical composition

Plate Tectonics

Choose the letter of the best answer.

1. What are the mechanisms that have been proposed to explain the movement of Earth's tectonic plates?

   A. slab pull and sea-floor spreading

   B. mantle convection and continental drift

   C. sea-floor spreading and continental drift

   D. mantle convection, ridge push, and slab pull

2. The movement of tectonic plates is so slow and gradual that you cannot see or feel them moving. As a result, scientists depend on the global positioning system (GPS) to verify tectonic plate motion. Satellites can measure the small distances that GPS ground stations move over time. In what units is the movement of tectonic plates measured?

   A. meters/day

   B. meters/week

   C. centimeters/year

   D. kilometers/month

3. Tectonic plates can be made of continental crust or oceanic crust, or a combination of the two. Besides their location, how else are these two kinds of crust **different**?

   A. Continental crust is thinner than oceanic crust.

   B. Continental crust is thicker than oceanic crust.

   C. Tectonic plates made of continental crust are larger than plates made of oceanic crust.

   D. Tectonic plates made of continental crust are smaller than plates made of oceanic crust.

4. A plate boundary is a place where two tectonic plates meet. There are several types of tectonic plate boundaries. Which statement below shows the correct definition of a tectonic plate boundary?

   A. At a divergent boundary, plates separate.

   B. At a transform boundary, plates move apart.

   C. At a convergent boundary, plates slide past each other.

   D. At a divergent boundary, one plate sinks under another plate.

5. The illustration below shows some of Earth's tectonic plates. The arrows indicate the direction in which some of these plates are moving.

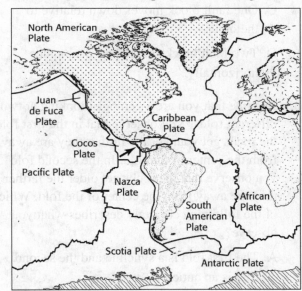

   According to this map, where can you infer that mountains are being formed?

   A. between the Scotia Plate and the Pacific Plate

   B. between the Cocos Plate and the Caribbean Plate

   C. between the South American Plate and the African Plate

   D. between the North America Plate and the Antarctic Plate

Mountain Building

Choose the letter of the best answer.

1. Over long periods of time, tectonic forces can cause rocks to fold. What kind of stress causes folding?

   A. tension

   B. shear stress

   C. compression

   D. normal stress

2. The San Andreas Fault in California is a strike-slip fault. Which of these statements best describes a strike-slip fault?

   A. Two fault blocks move in the same direction.

   B. One fault block moves up relative to the other.

   C. One fault block moves down relative to the other.

   D. Two fault blocks move past each other horizontally.

3. Imagine that you are a geologist looking at two different folds. You observe that in the first fold, the rocks get younger the farther they are away from the center of the fold. In the second fold you observe that the rocks get older the farther they are away from the center of the fold. Which of the following correctly describes what you observe?

   A. The first fold is a syncline and the second fold is an anticline.

   B. The first fold is an anticline and the second fold is a syncline.

   C. The first fold is a syncline and the second fold is a monocline.

   D. The first fold is an anticline and the second fold is a monocline.

4. This diagram shows the formation of fault-block mountains. The arrows show the direction of force. The curving line on the top of each figure depicts a river.

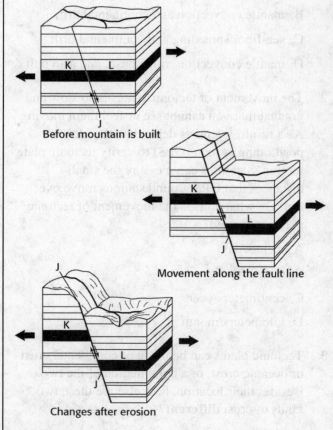

Before mountain is built

Movement along the fault line

Changes after erosion

   What does the letter *L* represent?

   A. the tension

   B. the footwall

   C. the fault line

   D. the hanging wall

5. What happens to rocks during deformation?

   A. Rocks become minerals.

   B. Rocks change shape and size.

   C. Rocks change into metal ores.

   D. Rocks change in mineral composition.

Volcanoes

Choose the letter of the best answer.

1. Which type of volcano has the steepest sides?

   A. shield

   B. composite

   C. pyroclastic

   D. cinder cone

2. What is the relationship between magma and lava?

   A. Magma is lava that has reached Earth's surface.

   B. Lava is magma that has reached Earth's surface.

   C. They are both types of solid material that spew out of a volcano.

   D. They are both molten rock found at different depths below Earth's surface.

3. A hot spot is a volcanically active area. A volcanic island can form over a hot spot. Which would you expect to find beneath the hot spot?

   A. a rift zone

   B. a mantle plume

   C. a divergent boundary

   D. a convergent boundary

4. How does pyroclastic material differ from lava?

   A. Unlike lava, pyroclastic material erupts onto Earth's surface.

   B. Unlike lava, pyroclastic material erupts from shield volcanoes.

   C. Unlike lava, pyroclastic material is associated with explosive eruptions.

   D. Unlike lava, pyroclastic material is associated with nonviolent eruptions.

5. The diagram below shows a cross section of a volcano.

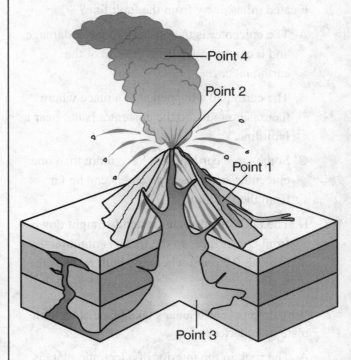

From which point would molten material, ash, and dust be expelled?

   A. point 1

   B. point 2

   C. point 3

   D. point 4

Earthquakes

Choose the letter of the best answer.

1. Many fault lines are obvious at the surface. How can the epicenter of an earthquake be located miles away from the fault line?

   A. The epicenter is the place of greatest damage, and it can be miles from the site of the earthquake.

   B. The earthquake happened at a place where there is no fault, so the epicenter is not near a fault line.

   C. Some large earthquakes have more than one epicenter, and these epicenters can be far from the fault line.

   D. The fault line does not extend straight down from the surface, so the focus is not directly beneath the point where the fault reaches the surface.

2. Why do most earthquakes take place at tectonic plate boundaries?

   A. The rock in the interior of a tectonic plate is stronger, so it does not deform.

   B. Earthquakes take place where the motion of tectonic plates transfers energy to rock.

   C. Earthquakes can only occur at places where magma can reach the surface and transfer energy to rocks.

   D. Earthquakes take place when one plate moves over another plate, which happens only at plate boundaries.

3. Which type of stress causes deformation that leads to earthquakes at converging plate boundaries?

   A. tension

   B. stretching

   C. shear stress

   D. compression

4. How does distance from the epicenter of an earthquake change the earthquake's effects?

   A. The strongest effects are at the epicenter.

   B. The strongest effects are felt furthest from the epicenter.

   C. The strongest effects are felt in a line extending north and south from the epicenter.

   D. The strongest effects are in a ring surrounding the epicenter with a radius of several miles.

5. On December 26, 2004, a major tsunami occurred in the Indian Ocean. The tsunami traveled from its point of origin to as far away as Africa—nearly 5,000 km. The map below shows the countries most affected by this tsunami.

December 2004 Tsunami

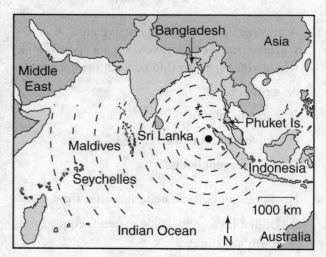

What was the cause of this tsunami?

   A. an earthquake beneath the ocean

   B. the impact of a large meteorite in the ocean

   C. a sudden violent windstorm above the ocean water

   D. a typhoon moving from the Indian Ocean toward India

Measuring Earthquake Waves

Choose the letter of the best answer.

1. Which of the following is the correct definition for the term *epicenter*?

   A. the position on Earth's surface where an earthquake begins

   B. the position along a fault directly below an earthquake's focus

   C. the position below Earth's surface where an earthquake begins

   D. the position on Earth's surface directly above an earthquake's focus

2. The graph shows the different arrival times for a P wave and an S wave at a seismometer.

   ### Measuring Earthquake Waves

   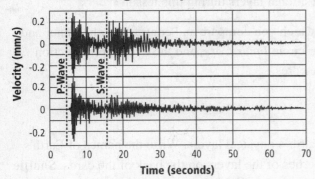

   How would the graph look differently if the earthquake had happened at a location that was farther away from the seismometer?

   A. The arrival times of both the P wave and the S wave would shift to the left.

   B. The arrival times of both the P wave and the S wave would shift to the right.

   C. The amount of time between the arrivals of the P and S waves would be longer.

   D. The amount of time between the arrivals of the P and S waves would be shorter.

3. What is the relationship between the intensity of an earthquake at a given location and the distance from the epicenter?

   A. Intensity increases with decreasing distance.

   B. Intensity decreases with decreasing distance.

   C. Intensity is not affected by changes in distance.

   D. Intensity remains constant with increasing distance.

4. Which of the following describes the moment magnitude of an earthquake?

   A. the amount of movement along a fault

   B. the distance from the earthquake's focus

   C. the amount of damage caused to buildings

   D. the distance from the earthquake's epicenter

5. P waves are also known as pressure waves. Which of the following correctly describes how P waves affect the rock through which they travel?

   A. circular or rolling motion parallel to the direction of travel

   B. side-to-side motion perpendicular to the direction of travel

   C. up-and-down motion perpendicular to the direction of travel

   D. compression and expansion parallel to the direction of travel

Earth's Layers

Take Your Pick: *Earth's Physical and Compositional Layers*
Complete the activities to show what you've learned about Earth's structure.

1. Work on your own, with a partner, or with a small group.

2. Choose items below for a total of 10 points. Check your choices.

3. Have your teacher approve your plan.

4. Submit or present your results.

2 Points

_____ **Picturing Earth's Layers** Create a poster that shows Earth's compositional layers. On the poster, label and briefly describe the three layers.

_____ **What Are Your Thoughts?** Make a card that answers the following questions: What did you know about Earth's compositional layers before completing this lesson? What was the most interesting thing you learned about Earth's compositional layers during this lesson?

_____ **Down to the Core** Make a Venn diagram in which you compare and contrast Earth's inner and outer cores. Label one circle *Outer Core*, the other circle *Inner Core*, and the overlapping section *Both*. Complete the diagram with details about the cores.

5 Points

_____ **The Layer Quiz** Make a quiz that deals with Earth's physical layers. Write the names of Earth's layers on note cards. Then write some of the properties of the layers on the back of the cards. Shuffle the cards and choose one from the pile. With a partner, take turns quizzing each other about the layers.

_____ **Seeing Inside** How do scientists know about Earth's interior? Find out more about how seismic waves and their speed help scientists learn about the inside of Earth. Present your findings in a visual presentation.

_____ **Your Turn to Teach** Suppose you are a teacher. Your task is to prepare a lesson about the layers of Earth. Gather information from your studies. Present your lesson to another student.

8 Points

_____ **Blast from the Past** Scientific understanding is constantly changing. Find out what scientists thought Earth was made of in the past. Make a timeline showing some past theories about Earth's internal structure.

_____ **What's in a Layer?** Make a multimedia presentation in which you compare and contrast the two ways of looking at Earth's internal structure.

Plate Tectonics

Climb the Pyramid: *Exploring Tectonic Plates*
Complete the activities to show what you have learned about plate tectonics.

1. Work on your own, with a partner, or with a small group.

2. Choose one item from each layer of the pyramid. Check your choices.

3. Have your teacher approve your plan.

4. Submit or present your results.

__ A Puzzling Picture

Create a drawing of the continents as they once fit together. Each continent should be a labeled and drawn in a different color. Carefully cut out each continent to create a puzzle. Then demonstrate the hypothesis of plate tectonics by moving the puzzle pieces and explaining the hypothesis and evidence to support it.

__ Plate Interview

Imagine that you are a newspaper reporter in 1912 who has heard about Alfred Wegener's astonishing new idea called continental drift. You are going to interview the scientist about his theory. List 10 questions to ask Wegener.

__ Sea-floor Spreading

Write a description of the process of sea-floor spreading, using the Mid-Atlantic Ridge as an example. Be sure to tell about how material reaches the surface and why the ridge is higher than the surrounding oceanic plates.

__ Density Differences

Write a poem or song that explains how density differences below Earth's plates causes the plates to move and change shape.

__ Flipbook

Draw a flipbook to show what happens at plate boundaries. Show a convergent boundary, a divergent boundary, and a transform boundary.

__ Collision Diorama

Make a diorama showing convergent boundaries formed between (1) two continental plates, (2) a continental plate and an oceanic plate, or (3) two oceanic plates. Create labels for your diorama.

Alternative Assessment

Mountain Building

Climb the Ladder: *Faults, Folds, and Mountains*
Complete the activities to show what you've learned about mountain building.

1. Work on your own, with a partner, or with a small group.

2. Choose one item from each rung of the ladder. Check your choices.

3. Have your teacher approve your plan.

4. Submit or present your results.

__ Quiz Cards On three separate cards, write the terms *compression*, *tension*, and *shear stress*. Then write their definitions on three other cards. Finally, mix up the cards and use them to quiz your friends about the terms.	**__ To a Fault** Make a poster that describes the three types of faults. Then draw a sketch of each type under the appropriate heading.
__ Flipping Forward Imagine that one of your classmates needs help understanding how folded mountains form. To help your classmate, create a flipbook that shows the process of a folded mountain forming.	**__ On the Range** Find out about a famous mountain range located anywhere in the world. Then share with the class what type of mountain range it is and the way it formed.
__ Plate Talk Imagine that you are a tectonic plate that is slowly pushing against another tectonic plate. Present a skit in which you describe what might happen to you and the other plate and why.	**__ You're the Expert!** Imagine you are a geologist who has examined a syncline fold. Write a report about what you observed in the field. In your report, note where the oldest rock is located in the fold and describe the shape of fold. Also discuss how the syncline occurred.

Volcanoes

Points of View: *Volcanoes and Volcanic Activity*
Your class will work together to show what you've learned about volcanoes from several different viewpoints.

1. Work in groups as assigned by your teacher. Each group will be assigned to one or two viewpoints.

2. Complete your assignment, and present your perspective to the class.

 Vocabulary Look up the root of the word *volcano*. Then find other words in the lesson that contain the same root. List these words, and write a definition for each.

 Illustrations Design trading cards for each type of volcano. On the cards draw images of and label all the types of volcanoes. Then describe how each type is different from or similar to other types of volcanoes.

 Analysis When volcanoes erupt, they release a number of different materials and change the landforms around them. Volcanoes can also change landforms by collapsing or exploding. How might Earth's surface be different if volcanoes did not exist? Which landforms and landmasses might not exist if it weren't for volcanoes? Create a PowerPoint presentation in which you describe your answers and ideas.

 Details Imagine that you have just watched a news report that stated that all volcanoes form at the boundaries of tectonic plates. Write a letter to the news station explaining that volcanoes can also form in other areas. Describe the other areas in which volcanoes form and explain how these volcanoes occur.

 Models Make a model of a shield volcano. Label the vent, the lava flow, and the magma chamber. Describe how a shield volcano is different from and similar to other types of volcanoes.

Earthquakes

Climb the Ladder: *Earthquake Exercises*
Complete the activities to show what you've learned about earthquakes.

1. Work on your own, with a partner, or with a small group.

2. Choose one item from each rung of the ladder. Check your choices.

3. Have your teacher approve your plan.

4. Submit or present your results.

__ **Earthquake Poster**	__ **Word Swap**
Make a poster that shows how an earthquake occurs. Label the focus, epicenter, and fault. Show how deformation can take place.	Choose one vocabulary word from this lesson. Write it at the bottom of a sheet of paper. Number each letter. Above the word, write a paragraph that tells something about the word. Then underline letters in your paragraph that are used in the word. Number these letters. Give your puzzle to partner. Have the partner use the numbers to figure out the word.
__ **Earthquake Events**	__ **Earthquake Article**
Create a flipchart that animates the sequence of events that causes an earthquake. Arrange you images into a book, so that when you flip the pages of the book, the earthquake causes the ground to move.	Suppose you are a reporter who experiences an earthquake. Write a magazine article about your experience. Describe what caused the quake, when it hit, what the aftermath was like, and how people's lives were affected.
__ **Shaky Story**	__ **Boundary Action**
Write a short story in which an earthquake occurs. What do your characters do? How do they react? What caused the earthquake?	Make models of a divergent boundary, a convergent boundary, and a transform plate boundary. Label the direction of plate movement.

Measuring Earthquake Waves

Alternative Assessment

Climb the Pyramid: *Research and Reporting*

Pretend you are a news reporter. In order to report on a fictional earthquake, you must develop your understanding of the causes of earthquakes, how they are measured, and their effects. You will execute a short research plan and then write a short newspaper article to report the details of this recent imaginary earthquake.

1. Work on your own.

2. Begin at the bottom of the pyramid. Choose one item from each layer and check your choices.

3. Have your teacher approve your plan.

4. Submit or present your results.

___ **Newspaper Article**

Write a newspaper article on a recent imaginary earthquake. Include a short background on earthquakes, then describe the earthquake's magnitude, intensity, and damages sustained in the community.

___ **Triangulation Map**

Review triangulation by researching different triangulation maps of previous earthquakes. Choose one map, and write a short summary describing how the epicenter of the earthquake is identified.

___ **Seismogram**

Review seismograms by researching several seismograms for past earthquakes. Choose one and write a short description of how lag times are used to determine an earthquake's magnitude.

___ **Earthquake Locations**

Research areas where earthquakes occur frequently. Write a short explanation of why earthquakes occur more frequently in certain locations.

___ **Before and After**

Make a picture collage or drawing that depicts the way a city or town looked before and after an earthquake. Cite any sources on the back.

___ **Lasting Construction**

Research construction materials, methods, and designs that can withstand strong shaking. Write a short recommendation for how to build in earthquake-prone areas.

Model Lava

Purpose In this activity, students will model lava flows to observe how a mixture's thickness affects how it flows and how easily gas escapes.

Time Period 45–60 minutes

Preparation Equip each station with the necessary materials. Have paper towels on hand to clean up any spills.

Safety Tips Have students review all safety icons before beginning this activity. Remind them never to eat or drink anything in the lab. Spilled water is a slipping hazard; clean up water spills immediately. Never work with electricity near water; be sure the floor and all work surfaces are dry. Students should not heat glassware that is broken, chipped, or cracked. They should use tongs or heat-resistant gloves to handle heated glassware and other equipment. Students should always wear heat-resistant gloves, goggles, and an apron when using a hot plate. Never leave a hot plate unattended while it is turned on. Allow all equipment to cool before storing it. Students should tie back long hair, secure loose clothing, and remove loose jewelry.

Teaching Strategies This activity works best with small groups. Because this activity is qualitative, measurements can be approximate instead of exact. After the activity, explain that volcanoes can erupt explosively because the magma inside is mostly made of silica, the basic building block of most minerals. Silica-rich magma is thick and stiff, flows slowly, and does not let water vapor and other gases easily escape. In fact, silica-rich magma tends to harden in the volcano, plugging it. If enough pressure builds up, the volcano could have an explosive eruption.

Magma that contains a smaller percentage of silica is thinner and runnier. Gases escape this type of magma easily, making it less likely that explosive pressures will build up.

Scoring Rubric

Possible points	Performance indicators
0–30	Lab technique
0–40	Quality and clarity of observations
0–30	Analysis

Model Lava

Objective

A mixture's thickness affects how quickly the mixture can flow. In this activity, you will model lava flows with different mixtures and discover how composition of lava affects its flow and its ability to trap gases.

Know the Score!

As you work through this activity, keep in mind that you will be earning a grade for the following:

- how well you work with the materials and equipment (30%)
- the quality of your observations (40%)
- the analysis of your observations (30%)

Materials and Equipment

- aluminum foil
- beakers, 400 mL (2)
- cornstarch, 20 mL
- gloves, heat resistant
- hot plate
- lab apron
- newspaper, 2 sheets

- pen, waterproof
- safety goggles
- stirring rod
- tape, masking, 20 cm
- tongs
- water, cold 500 mL

Safety Information

- Do not eat or drink anything in the laboratory.
- Clean up water spills immediately. Spilled water is a slipping hazard.

Procedure

1. Which will flow more slowly, a thick mixture or a thin one?

   _____

2. Which would allow more gas to escape, a thick mixture or a thin one?

   _____

3. Measure 5 mL of cornstarch into an empty beaker. Label the beaker "5 mL cornstarch" with masking tape.

4. Measure 15 mL of cornstarch into an empty beaker. Label the beaker "15 mL cornstarch" with masking tape.

5. Pout 250 mL of water into each beaker, and mix well.

6. Wearing goggles and heat-resistant gloves, plug in the hot plate and turn it on. Place a beaker on the hot plate.

7. Stir the mixture until it boils. Observe how much gas escapes. Are there many bubbles, some bubbles, or few bubbles? Remove the beaker from the hot plate.

8. Repeat Step 7 with the other beaker.

9. Turn off the hot plate. Using tongs, pour each mixture onto the center of a sheet of aluminum foil. Observe how each mixture spreads and flows. Do not touch the hot mixture.

Analysis

10. Describe the bubbles in each mixture. Which mixture had more bubbles? Which had fewer?

_____

11. Do thin or thick mixtures allow more gas to escape?

_____

12. Describe the flow of each mixture. Which mixture spread out more? Which spread out less? Explain the reason for each.

_____

_____

_____

_____

_____

_____

13. The cornstarch represents the mineral silica in lava. Based on your observations, how would a high-silica lava flow? How would a low-silica lava flow?

_____

_____

_____

14. Which type of lava would most likely plug a volcano?

_____

15. What can be said about the silica content in magma from a nonexplosive eruption?

_____

_____

_____

_____

Unit 4: The Restless Earth

Vocabulary

Fill in each blank with the term that best completes the following sentences.

1. The hot, convecting _____ is the layer of rock between the Earth's crust and core.

2. _____ is the theory that explains how large pieces of Earth's outermost layer move and change shape.

3. _____ is the bending of rock layers due to stress.

4. A(n) _____ is a vent or fissure in the Earth's surface through which magma and gases are expelled.

5. A(n) _____ is a movement or trembling of the ground that is caused by a sudden release of energy when rocks move along a fault.

Key Concepts

Read each question below, and circle the best answer.

6. What is the difference between lava and magma?

   A. Magma is found above Earth's surface and lava is found below Earth's surface.

   B. Lava is a solid material and magma is a liquid material.

   C. Magma is found below Earth's surface and lava is found above Earth's surface.

   D. Magma only erupts in the ocean and lava only erupts on land.

7. Tectonic plates are made of continental crust, oceanic crust, or a combination of the two. Besides their locations, how else are these two kinds of crust different?

   A. Tectonic plates made of continental crust are larger than plates made of oceanic crust.

   B. Tectonic plates made of continental crust are smaller than plates made of oceanic crust.

   C. Continental crust is thicker than oceanic plates.

   D. Continental crust is thinner than oceanic crust.

8. In the diagram below, an earthquake is taking place.

Cross Section of Lithosphere during an Earthquake

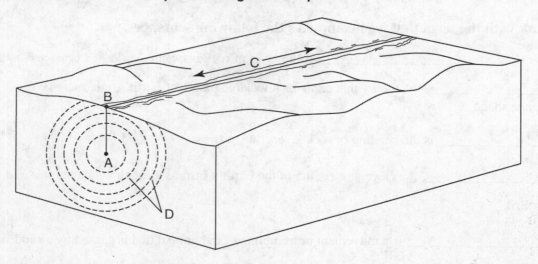

Where is the focus of the earthquake located?

A. Point A

B. Point B

C. along the line labeled C

D. along the series of circles labeled D

9. Volcanic eruptions can have many characteristics. They can be slow, fast, calm, explosive, or a combination of these. Which type of eruption is associated with the release of pyroclastic materials?

A. a calm eruption

B. an explosive eruption

C. a fast eruption

D. a slow eruption

10. What happens at a divergent tectonic plate boundary?

A. Two tectonic plates move horizontally past one another.

B. Two tectonic plates pull away from each other, forming a rift valley or mid-ocean ridge.

C. Two tectonic plates come together to form one plate.

D. Two tectonic plates collide, causing subduction.

11. A major tsunami occurred in the Indian Ocean on December 26, 2004 resulting in the loss of thousands of lives. The tsunami was caused by a major earthquake that originated below the point on the map on the ocean floor. The dashed lines on the map indicate the path of the tsunami's waves.

December 2004 Tsunami

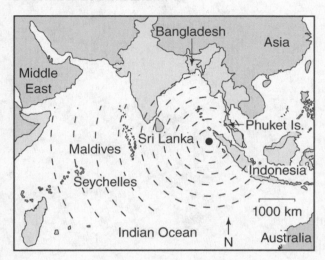

What term refers to the point on the ocean's surface indicated by the dot at the center of the waves?

A. fault boundary   C. earthquake epicenter

B. earthquake focus   D. tectonic plate boundary

12. Which of the following is a major difference between Earth's inner core and Earth's outer core?

A. the inner core is liquid and the outer core is solid

B. the inner core is solid and the outer core is liquid

C. the inner core is gas and the outer core is solid

D. the inner core is solid and the outer core is gas

13. Volcanic islands can form over hot spots. The Hawaiian Islands started forming over hot spots in the Pacific Ocean millions of years ago. What process causes the hot, solid rock to rise through the mantle at these locations?

A. condensation   C. convection

B. conduction   D. radiation

14. Earth's three compositional layers are the mantle, core, and crust.

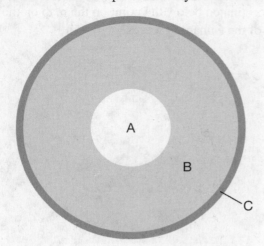

Which statement below is correct?

A. A is the crust, B is the core, and C is the mantle.

B. A is the core, B is the mantle, and C is the crust.

C. A is the inner core, B is the outer core, and C is the mantle.

D. A is the core, B is the crust, and C is the mantle.

15. Earth can be divided into five layers: lithosphere, asthenosphere, mesosphere, outer core, and inner core. Which properties are used to make these divisions?

A. compositional properties   C. chemical properties

B. physical properties   D. elemental properties

16. This diagram shows the formation of a fault-block mountain. Arrows outside of the blocks show the directions of force. Arrows inside the blocks show the directions of movement. The blocks *K* and *L* move along a line marked *J*.

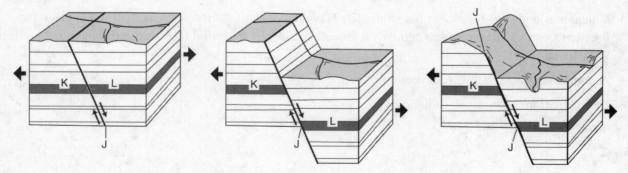

What does the line marked by the letter *J* represent?

A. a river   C. the fault line

B. a rock layer   D. the focus

17. The map below shows the epicenters of some major earthquakes of 2003.

Locations of Major Earthquakes in 2003

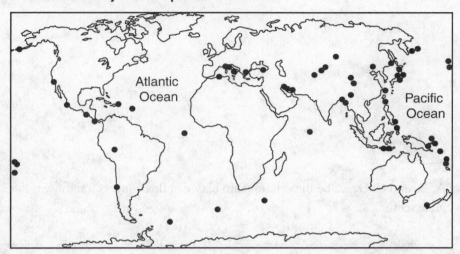

What is the most likely reason that there were no major earthquakes recorded in the interior of the continent of Africa?

A. There are no faults in Africa.

B. The landmass of Africa is too large to be affected by earthquakes.

C. The plate boundary inside Africa is too small to form earthquakes.

D. No major plate boundaries cut through the continent of Africa.

Critical Thinking
Answer the following questions in the space provided.

18. Explain how a convergent boundary is different from a transform boundary. Then, name one thing that commonly occurs along both convergent boundaries and transform boundaries.

_____

_____

_____

_____

_____

19. The diagram below shows the five physical layers of Earth.

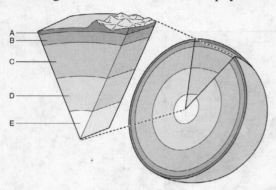

Identify the physical layers A, B, and C. Describe the relationship between these layers and how it is important to understanding plate tectonics.

_____

_____

_____

_____

20. Explain the difference between the Richter scale and the Moment Magnitude scale. Why might measurements from the Richter Scale be misleading to someone who does not know how it works?

_____

_____

_____

_____

_____

Connect ESSENTIAL QUESTIONS

Lessons 3 and 4

Answer the following question in the space provided.

21. Explain how forces from tectonic plate movement can build these three types of mountains: folded mountains, fault-block mountains, and volcanic mountains.

_____

_____

_____

_____

_____

The Restless Earth

Key Concepts
Choose the letter of the best answer.

1. Most tectonic plates have both oceanic and continental crust. How are oceanic and continental crust different?

    A. Oceanic crust is thinner and lighter than continental crust.

    B. Oceanic crust is thicker and lighter than continental crust.

    C. Oceanic crust is thinner and denser than continental crust.

    D. Oceanic crust is thicker and denser than continental crust.

2. Which of the following defines magma?

    A. Magma is lava that has cooled to form solid rock.

    B. Magma is molten rock that flows on Earth's surface.

    C. Magma is melted rock found in underground chambers.

    D. Magma is any place where gas, ash, or melted rock come out of the ground.

3. During the year 2003, the number of earthquakes that occurred was higher than usual. The map below shows the locations of some of these earthquakes.

Locations of Major Earthquakes in 2003

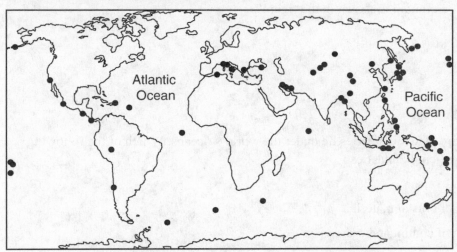

Where did the highest concentration of earthquakes occur?

    A. within the ocean basins

    B. within the continental landmasses

    C. along the edges of the Pacific Ocean

    D. along the edges of the Atlantic Ocean

4. Pyroclastic flows are the most dangerous type of volcanic eruption. Extremely hot gases and fragments of rock travel at speeds over 100 km per hour. Which type of volcano is made mostly of pyroclastic materials?

   A. lava

   B. shield

   C. composite

   D. cinder cone

5. The figure below shows mountains that were formed when large blocks of rock were squeezed together as two tectonic plates collided.

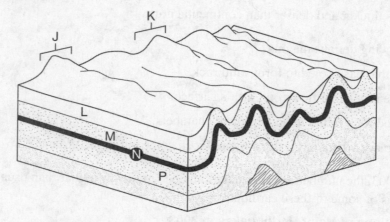

   What kind of mountain is shown in the figure?

   A. folded

   B. eroded

   C. volcanic

   D. fault block

6. Most divergent plate boundaries lie under the world's oceans. Which of the following is a process that occurs at divergent boundaries?

   A. magnetic reversals

   B. recycling of crustal material

   C. formation of continental crust

   D. formation of mid-ocean ridges

7. The figure below shows three kinds of faults: a normal fault, a reverse fault, and a strike-slip fault.

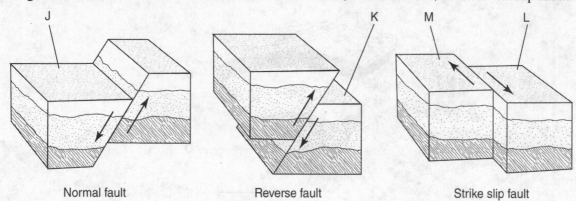

Normal fault   Reverse fault   Strike slip fault

What happens when stress causes a normal fault?

A. The footwall drops down.

B. The hanging wall moves up.

C. The walls move side to side.

D. The hanging wall drops down.

8. The effects of an earthquake depend on many factors, not just the amount of energy released at the focus. Which types of buildings would best be able to withstand the effects of an earthquake?

A. taller buildings made of steel or wood

B. shorter buildings made of steel or wood

C. taller buildings made of brick or concrete

D. shorter buildings made of brick or concrete

9. Volcanic vents are places where magma can erupt onto Earth's surface. Which volcanic feature forms a relatively small depression around a volcano's vent?

A. crater

B. fissure

C. caldera

D. lava plateau

10. Two types of seismic waves are body waves and surface waves. What is the main difference between body waves and surface waves?

A. Body waves travel in all directions, and surface waves travel in only one direction.

B. Surface waves travel in all directions, and body waves travel in only one direction.

C. Body waves travel outward from the focus, and surface waves travel only on the surface.

D. Surface waves travel outward from the focus, and body waves travel only on the surface.

11. Earth has five layers based on physical characteristics. The diagram below shows these five layers.

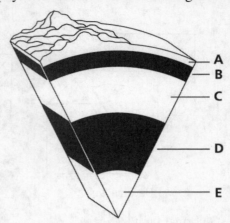

Which letter represents the asthenosphere, the soft layer on which the tectonic plates move?

A. A

B. B

C. C

D. D

12. What causes an earthquake to happen?

A. Surface rocks move suddenly as a result of physical stress.

B. Rocks along an underground fault move suddenly and release energy.

C. Large amounts of rock suddenly shift downward when large holes form under them.

D. Energy is transferred to rock layers from convection currents in the oceans and the atmosphere.

13. Scientists divide Earth into three main layers: the core, the mantle, and the crust. How are these three layers identified?

A. by their plate tectonics

B. by their structural features

C. by their physical properties

D. by their chemical composition

14. Long ago the eastern part of North America collided with the northern part of Africa during the formation of the supercontinent Pangaea. Later, the two continents separated as Pangaea broke apart. Which of the following describes what happened when the two continents collided?

A. Folded mountains formed as a result of tensional stress.

B. Fault-block mountains formed as a result of tensional stress.

C. Folded mountains formed as a result of compressional stress.

D. Fault-block mountains formed as a result of compressional stress.

15. The figure below shows the process of subduction.

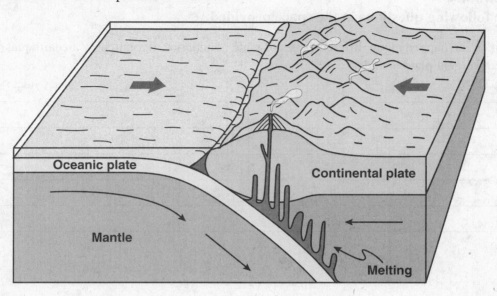

What happens when the crustal plates move as shown in the figure?

A. An ocean forms.

B. Volcanic mountain ranges form.

C. Sea-floor spreading occurs as the oceanic plate moves.

D. A transform boundary forms where the subduction occurs.

Critical Thinking

Answer the following questions in the space provided.

16. Earthquakes can happen along different types of plate boundaries. Explain how an earthquake takes place along a convergent plate boundary.

   _____

   _____

   _____

   _____

   _____

   _____

Extended Response
Answer the following questions in the space provided.

17. Earth's core is divided into two physical layers, the inner core and the outer core. Both are made mostly of iron and nickel. However, scientists think that the inner core rotates at a slightly faster rate than the rest of the planet. Explain the main difference between the inner and outer cores. Then describe how this difference could explain why the rotation speeds are different.

_____

_____

_____

_____

_____

_____

The Restless Earth

Key Concepts
Choose the letter of the best answer.

1. Most tectonic plates have both oceanic and continental crust. How are oceanic and continental crust different?

   A. Oceanic crust is heavier because it has more iron and magnesium than continental crust has.

   B. Oceanic crust is lighter because it has more iron and magnesium than continental crust has.

   C. Oceanic crust is heavier because it has more silicon and aluminum than continental crust has.

   D. Oceanic crust is lighter because it has more silicon and aluminum than continental crust has.

2. Which of the following describes magma?

   A. solid rock

   B. molten rock

   C. volcanic ash

   D. volcanic cone

3. During the year 2003, the number of earthquakes that occurred was higher than usual. The map below shows the locations of some of these earthquakes.

Locations of Major Earthquakes in 2003

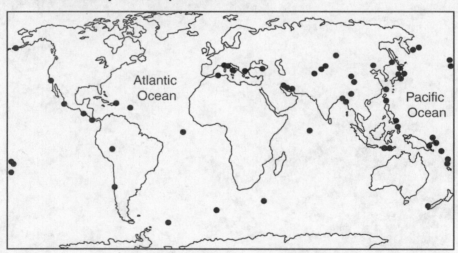

   Why do the dots on the map tend to form a long curving line in the western part of the Pacific Ocean?

   A. This part of the ocean has a high rate of hurricanes and typhoons.

   B. That part of the ocean is directly above the boundaries between tectonic plates.

   C. An increase in the number of tsunamis in the Pacific led to an increase in the number of earthquakes.

   D. There is pressure on the sea floor due to the weight of water of the Pacific Ocean.

4. Pyroclastic flows are the most dangerous type of volcanic eruption. Extremely hot gases and fragments of rock travel at speeds over 100 km per hour. Which type of volcano is least likely to have a pyroclastic flow?

   A. lava

   B. shield

   C. composite

   D. cinder cone

5. The figure below shows mountains that were formed when large blocks of rock were squeezed together as two tectonic plates collided.

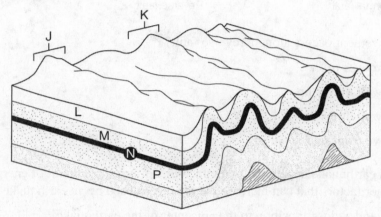

   What does the letter *K* represent?

   A. syncline

   B. anticline

   C. oldest rock

   D. newest rock

6. Most divergent plate boundaries lie under the world's oceans. Which of the following is a process that occurs at divergent boundaries?

   A. subduction of old crust

   B. formation of new crust

   C. plates slide past each other

   D. continental collisions occur

7. The figure below shows three kinds of faults: normal faults, reverse faults, and strike-slip faults.

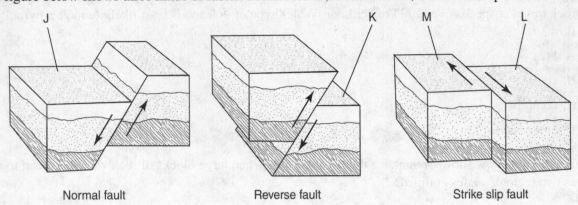

Normal fault   Reverse fault   Strike slip fault

What kind of movement occurs along a reverse fault?

A. The footwall moves up.

B. The hanging wall moves up.

C. The hanging wall drops down.

D. The walls move from side to side.

8. The effects of an earthquake depend on many factors, not just the amount of energy released at the focus. What are two other factors that can increase the damage caused by an earthquake?

A. solid bedrock and a closer position to the epicenter of the earthquake

B. sediments that contain water and a shallower depth of the earthquake's focus

C. steep slopes and a position that is farther from the epicenter of the earthquake

D. loose sediments and an earthquake focus that is at a greater depth below the surface

9. Volcanic vents are places where magma can erupt onto Earth's surface. In some cases, these vents are long cracks in the ground. What is this type of crack in Earth's surface called?

A. crater

B. fissure

C. caldera

D. lava plateau

10. Two types of seismic waves are body waves and surface waves. Which of the following statements correctly describes body waves and surface waves?

A. Body waves include P waves and S waves, which travel faster than surface waves travel.

B. Surface waves include P waves and S waves, which travel faster than body waves travel.

C. Body waves include P waves, which are the faster waves, and surface waves include S waves, which are slower.

D. Surface waves include P waves, which are the faster waves, and body waves include S waves, which are slower.

11. Earth has five layers based on physical properties. The diagram below shows these five layers.

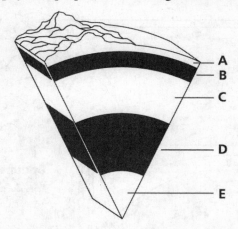

Which letter represents the mesosphere?

A. B

B. C

C. D

D. E

12. Which of the following events can produce an earthquake?

A. the force of tsunamis in the oceans

B. movement of tectonic plates along a fault

C. a sudden release of energy from the mantle

D. the violent shaking of sections of the lithosphere

13. Scientists divide Earth into three main layers. Each layer has a different chemical composition. Which is the innermost layer of Earth?

A. Earth's innermost layer is the core.

B. Earth's innermost layer is the mantle.

C. Earth's innermost layer is the lithosphere.

D. Earth's innermost layer is the asthenosphere.

14. Long ago the eastern part of North America collided with the northern part of Africa during the formation of the supercontinent Pangaea. Later, the two continents separated as Pangaea broke apart. Which of the following describes what happened when the two continents separated?

A. Folded mountains formed as a result of tensional stress.

B. Fault-block mountains formed as a result of tensional stress.

C. Folded mountains formed as a result of compressional stress.

D. Fault-block mountains formed as a result of compressional stress.

15. The figure below shows the process of subduction.

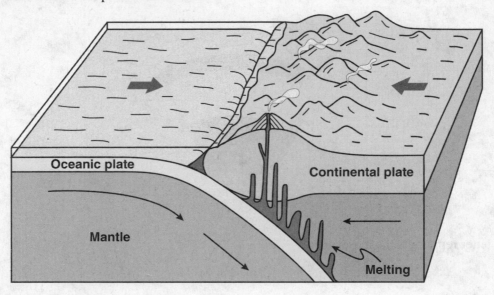

What can you conclude from this figure?

A. The two tectonic plates are sliding past each other horizontally along Earth's surface.

B. The two tectonic plates are moving apart to create a mid-ocean ridge on the sea floor.

C. The two tectonic plates are converging so that a mountain range forms on the continent.

D. The two tectonic plates are diverging causing the continental plate to buckle and form mountains.

Critical Thinking

Answer the following questions in the space provided.

16. Earthquakes can happen along different types of plate boundaries. Explain how an earthquake takes place along a transform plate boundary.

_____

_____

_____

_____

_____

_____

Name _____ Date _____

Extended Response
Answer the following questions in the space provided.

17. Earth's core is divided into two physical layers, the inner core and the outer core. Both are made mostly of iron and nickel. However, the layers are very different. Explain the main difference between these two layers. Then design a simple demonstration or model to show the main difference between the inner core and outer core, and explain.

_____

_____

_____

_____

_____

_____

_____

The Dynamic Earth

Choose the letter of the best answer.

1. Which of the following are body waves?

   A. P waves and S waves

   B. P waves and Richter waves

   C. Richter waves and S waves

   D. surface waves and P waves

2. Isabella went hiking with her family near a river valley. They noticed that they were walking on a yellowish-gray sediment. Isabella pointed out that it was called loess and then correctly explained how it formed. Which could be Isabella's explanation?

   A. Layers of rock were deposited on one another.

   B. Layers of dust were deposited by wind and built up.

   C. Layers of sediment were deposited by moving rivers.

   D. Layers of ice were deposited by snow and turned into ice.

3. Gopher tortoises live on dry land. They live in large holes that they dig in the soil. How does the behavior of the gopher tortoise cause physical weathering?

   A. It loosens the soil, allowing more water to reach the rocks underground.

   B. It erodes the soil by moving it from underneath the ground to above ground.

   C. It moves rocks above ground, where they are exposed to more water and wind.

   D. It causes exfoliation of the rocks as the tortoise breaks the rocks into smaller pieces.

4. Derrick started to create a flow chart to show how one kind of rock can change into metamorphic rock.

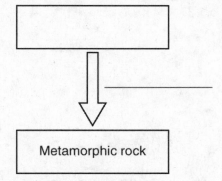

   Which of these rock types could Derrick include in the top box?

   A. igneous rock only

   B. sedimentary rock only

   C. either igneous rock or sedimentary rock

   D. neither igneous rock nor sedimentary rock

5. Phong is examining samples of quartz, feldspar, and mica. What do all of these samples have in common?

   A. They are metals.

   B. They are pure elements.

   C. They are silicate minerals.

   D. They are nonsilicate minerals.

6. Tectonic plates can move, as shown in the figure below.

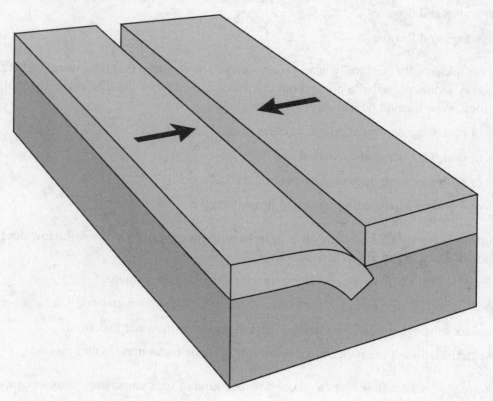

   What does this figure show?

   A. a divergent boundary

   B. a transform boundary

   C. a convergent boundary

   D. a stationary plate boundary

7. How does sedimentary rock usually form?

   A. in large crystals

   B. in vertical layers

   C. in swirling bands

   D. in horizontal layers

8. It can take a long time for soil to form. Which are the primary factors that affect soil formation?

   A. rainfall, temperature, wind, time, and plants

   B. time, climate, topography, plants, and animals

   C. parent rock, sunshine, plants, animals, and bacteria

   D. climate, parent rock, topography, living things, and time

9. Which is a cause of chemical weathering?

   A. ice

   B. wind

   C. oxygen

   D. gravity

10. A mineral sample contains 25% of its original amount of potassium-40. The diagram below represents how potassium-40 decays.

Decay of Potassium-40

	1.3 billion years		1.3 billion years		1.3 billion years	
100%	→	50%	→	25%	→	12.5%

How long ago did the mineral form?

   A. 1.3 million years

   B. 2.6 million years

   C. 1.3 billion years

   D. 2.6 billion years

11. The San Andreas Fault System in Northern California has produced many strong earthquakes over the past two centuries. The graph below shows the strongest of the earthquakes along this fault system. The number to the right of the year indicates the magnitude of the earthquake. A greater number corresponds to a stronger earthquake.

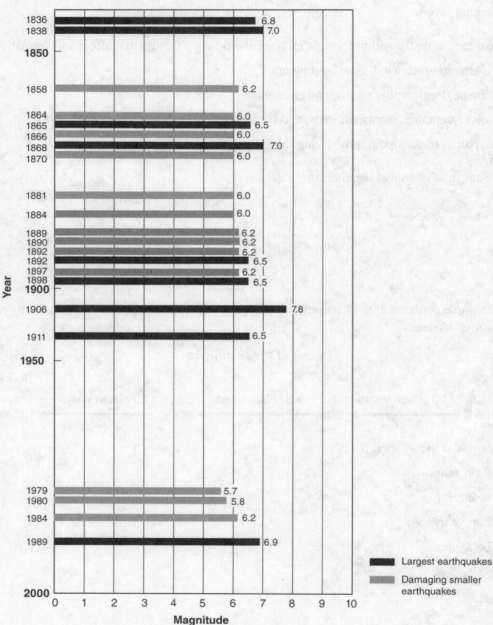

Earthquakes in Northern California

Year	Magnitude
1836	6.8
1838	7.0
1850	
1858	6.2
1864	6.0
1865	6.5
1866	6.0
1868	7.0
1870	6.0
1881	6.0
1884	6.0
1889	6.2
1890	6.2
1892	6.2
1892	6.5
1897	6.2
1898	6.5
1900	
1906	7.8
1911	6.5
1950	
1979	5.7
1980	5.8
1984	6.2
1989	6.9
2000	

■ Largest earthquakes
▬ Damaging smaller earthquakes

What was happening during the time between these earthquakes?

A. Energy built up as stress in the rock due to plate motion.

B. Energy stored in the rock decreased due to elastic rebound.

C. The fault closed, so there was very little energy to cause an earthquake.

D. The energy stored in the rock decreased as tectonic plates moved apart.

12. What is the term for the place where land and a body of water meet?

    A. a delta

    B. a shoreline

    C. groundwater

    D. an alluvial fan

13. Which of these answers describes Earth's atmosphere?

    A. all living and once-living things

    B. the mixture of gases that surrounds Earth

    C. a mixture of nickel and iron below the mantle

    D. all the salt and fresh liquid water on Earth's surface

14. The table shows layers of rock found in two areas, listed from the top layer (rock layer 1) to the bottom layer (rock layer 5). It shows the rock types (W, X, Y, Z) and the fossils (T and U) found in each layer. The rocks in area 1 are undisturbed. The rocks in area 2 are disturbed and completely overturned.

Rock Layer	Area 1	Area 2
1	rock X	rock Z
2	rock Y	fossil T
3	fossil T	rock Y
4	rock Z	rock X
5	rock W	fossil U

Which rock layer is the youngest?

    A. rock layer 1 in area 1

    B. rock layer 5 in area 1

    C. rock layer 1 in area 2

    D. rock layer 5 in area 2

15. Scientists think the continents once formed a large, single landmass that broke apart, and then the continents slowly drifted to their present locations. What is the name given to this hypothesis?

    A. continental rise

    B. continental drift

    C. continental shelf

    D. continental slope

16. At one time, several kinds of camels lived in Florida. The evidence comes from fossils found in Florida. Which of these objects would be a fossil that shows that camels once lived in Florida?

   A. sinkhole formed by a retreating glacier

   B. sedimentary rock that formed a long time ago

   C. crystal formation suspended from the ceiling of a cave

   D. remains of an organism preserved by geologic processes

17. Which kind of material would flow onto Earth's surface during a nonexplosive volcanic eruption?

   A. lava

   B. magma

   C. composite

   D. pyroclastic

18. Look at the features of the valley in the following picture.

How was this valley formed?

A. A continental glacier retreated, pushing sediment to the side.

B. An alpine glacier flowed down through the valley, causing erosion.

C. An alpine glacier dragged huge blocks of ice that formed kettle lakes.

D. A continental glacier flowed through the valley, depositing glacial drift.

19. Earth is divided into compositional layers based on chemical composition. Which compositional layer is a hot, convecting layer of rock?

    A. core

    B. plate

    C. crust

    D. mantle

20. Which of the following gives a correct description of lava and magma?

    A. Lava is magma that erupts onto Earth's surface.

    B. Lava is hot, liquid rock and magma is solidified lava.

    C. Lava forms intrusive rocks and magma forms extrusive rocks.

    D. Lava forms foliated rocks and magma forms nonfoliated rocks.

21. You have just analyzed a 100 g soil sample. You have organized your findings in the following data table:

Soil Analysis	
Soil Material	Amount (by % volume)
Air	25
Silt	18
Clay	9
Sand	18
Water	25
Organic matter	5

Which two materials make up at least 50 percent of the composition of your soil sample?

    A. air and silt

    B. silt and sand

    C. air and water

    D. clay and organic matter

22. What is the approximate age of Earth?

    A. 4.6 billion years

    B. 4.6 million years

    C. 46,000 years

    D. 4,600 years

23. During which division of geologic time did the continents come together to form the supercontinent Pangaea?

A. Cenozoic Era

B. Paleozoic Era

C. Triassic Period

D. Jurassic Period

24. During the year 2003, a greater number of earthquakes took place than is usually recorded per year. The map below shows the locations of some major earthquakes of 2003.

Locations of Major Earthquakes in 2003

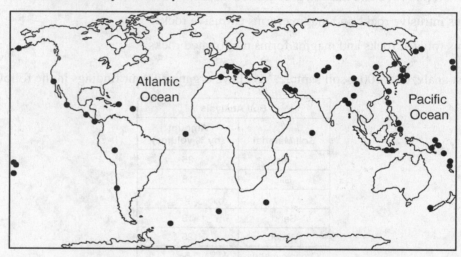

What is the most likely reason that there were no major earthquakes recorded in the interior of the continent of Africa?

A. There are no faults in Africa

B. The plate boundary inside Africa is too small to form earthquakes.

C. The landmass of Africa is too great to be affected by earthquakes.

D. The entire continent of Africa is located on a single continental tectonic plate.

25. Earth's physical layers correspond to Earth's compositional layers. Which part of the mantle is also part of the lithosphere?

A. the fluid, hot part

B. the rigid upper part

C. the soft moving part

D. the lower stationary part

26. Which of the following can form as a result of tension caused by tectonic plate movement?

    A. a syncline

    B. an anticline

    C. a folded mountain

    D. a fault-block mountain

27. The following diagram shows the site of a sinkhole.

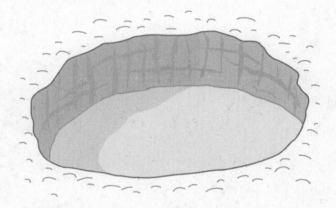

Which landform was most likely present before the sinkhole formed?

    A. a cave

    B. a canyon

    C. a shallow pond

    D. a deep river valley

28. Volcanic islands can form over hot spots. The Hawaiian Islands started forming over a hot spot in the Pacific Ocean millions of years ago. What process causes the hot, solid rock to rise through the mantle at these locations?

    A. radiation

    B. conduction

    C. convection

    D. condensation

Name ______________________________________ Date _________

29. Earth has both fresh water and saltwater. About how much of Earth's water is fresh water?

A. 3%

B. 15%

C. 67%

D. 97%

30. Erosion is a process that slowly changes rocks. Which of the following most likely causes pebbles in a stream to erode?

A. flowing water

B. force of gravity

C. movement of ice

D. freezing and thawing

Name _____ Date _____

PLEASE NOTE

- Use only a no. 2 pencil
- Example: Ⓐ ● Ⓒ Ⓓ
- Erase changes COMPLETELY.

End-of-Module Test

Mark one answer for each question.

1 Ⓐ Ⓑ Ⓒ Ⓓ   11 Ⓐ Ⓑ Ⓒ Ⓓ   21 Ⓐ Ⓑ Ⓒ Ⓓ

2 Ⓐ Ⓑ Ⓒ Ⓓ   12 Ⓐ Ⓑ Ⓒ Ⓓ   22 Ⓐ Ⓑ Ⓒ Ⓓ

3 Ⓐ Ⓑ Ⓒ Ⓓ   13 Ⓐ Ⓑ Ⓒ Ⓓ   23 Ⓐ Ⓑ Ⓒ Ⓓ

4 Ⓐ Ⓑ Ⓒ Ⓓ   14 Ⓐ Ⓑ Ⓒ Ⓓ   24 Ⓐ Ⓑ Ⓒ Ⓓ

5 Ⓐ Ⓑ Ⓒ Ⓓ   15 Ⓐ Ⓑ Ⓒ Ⓓ   25 Ⓐ Ⓑ Ⓒ Ⓓ

6 Ⓐ Ⓑ Ⓒ Ⓓ   16 Ⓐ Ⓑ Ⓒ Ⓓ   26 Ⓐ Ⓑ Ⓒ Ⓓ

7 Ⓐ Ⓑ Ⓒ Ⓓ   17 Ⓐ Ⓑ Ⓒ Ⓓ   27 Ⓐ Ⓑ Ⓒ Ⓓ

8 Ⓐ Ⓑ Ⓒ Ⓓ   18 Ⓐ Ⓑ Ⓒ Ⓓ   28 Ⓐ Ⓑ Ⓒ Ⓓ

9 Ⓐ Ⓑ Ⓒ Ⓓ   19 Ⓐ Ⓑ Ⓒ Ⓓ   29 Ⓐ Ⓑ Ⓒ Ⓓ

10 Ⓐ Ⓑ Ⓒ Ⓓ   20 Ⓐ Ⓑ Ⓒ Ⓓ   30 Ⓐ Ⓑ Ⓒ Ⓓ

Test Doctor

Unit 1 Earth's Surface

Unit Pretest

1. B 5. C 9. B
2. D 6. C 10. C
3. B 7. B
4. C 8. C

1. B

A is incorrect because although alpine glaciers form U-shaped valleys from V-shaped valleys, continental glaciers form flattened landscapes, not V-shaped valleys.

B is correct because alpine glaciers form rugged landscapes, and continental glaciers form flat landscapes.

C is incorrect because alpine glaciers form rugged landscapes, and continental glaciers form flat landscapes.

D is incorrect because alpine glaciers form rugged landscapes, and continental glaciers form flat landscapes.

2. D

A is incorrect because dunes are gently sloped on the side where the wind blows and have a steep slope on the other side as sand drops over the edge of the dune.

B is incorrect because dunes are gently sloped on the side where the wind blows and have a steep slope on the other side as sand drops over the edge of the dune.

C is incorrect because dunes are gently sloped on the side where the wind blows and have a steep slope on the other side as sand drops over the edge of the dune. The wind direction of arrow Q would not form a sand dune.

D is correct because dunes are gently sloped on the side where the wind blows and have a steep slope on the other side as sand drops over the edge of the dune.

3. B

A is incorrect because the biosphere includes all living and once-living things.

B is correct because the frozen water of an ice sheet is part of the cryosphere.

C is incorrect because the atmosphere is composed of a mixture of gases.

D is incorrect because the hydrosphere is liquid water.

4. C

A is incorrect because a river delta is the same shape but forms where a river meets an ocean or sea.

B is incorrect because the diagram shows an alluvial fan, not a floodplain.

C is correct because an alluvial fan is a fan-shaped deposit of sediment formed where a fast-flowing river or stream reaches a flatter area of land.

D is incorrect because an oxbow lake is formed when a bend in the river is cut off.

5. C

A is incorrect because waves depositing debris on the island would not remove sand from the island but would leave behind sand.

B is incorrect because currents may move sand along the island, but waves crashing over it are the main reason that sand is removed.

C is correct because barrier islands can change significantly during storms as waves crash over the island and remove sand from the island.

D is incorrect because waves crashing over barrier islands are a greater cause of sand removal than strong winds.

6. C

A is incorrect because acid in decaying leaves cannot displace soil to expose rock.

B is incorrect because acids increase chemical weathering of rock.

C is correct because acids are agents of chemical weathering, and decaying leaves add organic matter to soil.

D is incorrect because chemical weathering and soil formation occur more rapidly when soil is more acidic.

7. B

A is incorrect because air is an agent of chemical weathering, but not physical weathering.

B is correct because wind causes abrasion but is not an agent of physical weathering.

C is incorrect because acids are agents of chemical weathering, but not physical weathering.

D is incorrect because water is an agent of both chemical and physical weathering.

8. C

A is incorrect because iron accounts for about 5% of Earth's crust.

B is incorrect because very little nickel is found in Earth's crust.

C is correct because more than half of Earth's crust is oxygen and silicates, which contain oxygen.

D is incorrect because aluminum is an element in Earth's crust, but it is not the most abundant element.

9. B

A is incorrect because that is not the lowest point on the graph.

B is correct because that is the point with the lowest amount of rainfall, so it will have the least weathering.

C is incorrect because the point for the average rainfall in Miami in January is lower than for Gainesville in June.

D is incorrect because that is the point for the average rainfall in Miami in January, and it is lower than Gainesville in October.

10. C

A is incorrect because the A horizon is the top layer of soil in a typical soil profile; it contains the most humus, which is an important kind of organic matter.

B is incorrect because the B horizon typically contains less organic matter than the A horizon but more than the C horizon.

C is correct because the C horizon is the bottom layer of soil in a typical soil profile; it contains mostly weathered rock and little to no organic matter.

D is incorrect because the O horizon refers to the layer of decaying organic matter that covers soil but is not part of the soil itself.

Lesson 1 Quiz

1. D   4. D
2. C   5. C
3. C

1. D

A is incorrect because the geosphere is the rocky, solid part of Earth.

B is incorrect because the cryosphere is Earth's water in its solid (frozen) form.

C is incorrect because the atmosphere is the mixture of gases that surrounds Earth.

D is correct because the hydrosphere is the liquid water on Earth, which includes the water in wetlands.

2. C

A is incorrect because oxygen is not part of the biosphere, which consists only of living things.

B is incorrect because the oxygen that organisms breathe is not part of the geosphere.

C is correct because the oxygen that organisms breathe is part of the atmosphere that surrounds Earth.

D is incorrect because the oxygen that birds breathe is not part of the hydrosphere.

3. C

A is incorrect because rain is part of the hydrosphere.

B is incorrect because lakes are part of the hydrosphere.

C is correct because permafrost and icebergs are solid forms of water, which make up the cryosphere.

D is incorrect because rainfall is part of the hydrosphere.

4. D

A is incorrect because the interaction of the geosphere (rocky Earth and its layers) and bio-sphere (living things) do not cause waves and currents to form.

B   is incorrect because the interaction of the biosphere (living things) and hydrosphere (liquid water) do not cause waves and currents to form.

C   is incorrect because the interaction of the cryosphere (frozen water) and atmosphere (gases surrounding Earth) do not cause waves and currents to form.

D   is correct because the sun's energy in the atmosphere (gases surrounding Earth) creates wind, and the interaction of wind and the hydrosphere (liquid water) produces waves and surface currents.

5. C

A   is incorrect because mountains are not a source of energy for the whole of Earth's biosphere.

B   is incorrect because trees are part of Earth's living things and are a source of energy for some things but are not their own source of energy.

C   is correct because all of Earth's living things derive their energy, ultimately, from the sun.

D   is incorrect because storms and lightning do not provide energy to living things.

Lesson 2 Quiz
1. A   4. A
2. B   5. C
3. D

1. A

A   is correct because weathering is the process by which rocks are broken down by physical and chemical means.

B   is incorrect because erosion is the process that moves rocks.

C   is incorrect because weathering breaks down rocks.

D   is incorrect because weathering breaks down rocks, but does not change them into a different type of rock.

2. B

A   is incorrect because pebble 1 had more abrasion, so it was more easily worn away and is softer.

B   is correct because pebble 2 did not wear away as easily as pebble 1, so it is harder.

C   is incorrect because the rate of abrasion does not depend on the chemical properties of the rock.

D   is incorrect because the rate of abrasion is a physical process, not a chemical process.

3. D

A   is incorrect because chemical weathering does not lead to the formation of crystals.

B   is incorrect because rocks may react with acids but do not usually produce acids when they are weathered.

C   is incorrect because chemical weathering wears away the rock, and stronger rock would be more difficult to wear away.

D   is correct because the chemical composition of the rock changes, and the substances usually crumble more easily than the original rock.

4. A

A   is correct because plant roots and ice wedging can cause cracks in rocks to grow over time.

B   is incorrect because wind abrasion does not cause cracks in rocks to grow.

C   is incorrect because animal burrowing does not cause cracks in rocks to grow.

D   is incorrect because animal burrowing and wind abrasion do not widen cracks in rocks.

5. C

A   is incorrect because acids are not an agent of physical weathering.

B   is incorrect because acids would not decrease physical actions that lead to weathering.

C   is correct because acids are agents of chemical weathering, and the decaying leaves will make the soil more acidic.

D   is incorrect because chemical weathering happens more quickly in more acidic conditions.

Lesson 3 Quiz

1. A   4. D
2. D   5. C
3. B

1. A

A is correct because erosion is defined as the movement of soil or sediment from one place to another.

B is incorrect because the term *discharge* refers to the amount of water in a water body.

C is incorrect because deposition describes the soil being laid down, and the correct term for the movement of soil from one place to another is erosion.

D is incorrect because weathering is defined as the breakdown of rocks.

2. D

A is incorrect because not all liquid water is groundwater, but only water below Earth's surface.

B is incorrect because groundwater is defined as water below Earth's surface and can be moving.

C is incorrect because groundwater is defined as water below Earth's surface, not water on Earth's surface.

D is correct because groundwater is defined as water below Earth's surface (collected and stored underground).

3. B

A is incorrect because deep valleys in the mountains are commonly caused by streams rather than earthquakes.

B is correct because as streams flow through the mountains, the running water causes erosion and a deep valley forms.

C is incorrect because deep valleys in the mountains are commonly caused by streams, not rock landslides.

D is incorrect because the most likely cause is erosion by water, not erosion by wind.

4. D

A is incorrect because the appearance of coarse sand and pebbles in the sediment indicate a higher rate of erosion after a storm.

B is incorrect because the sediment flowing in the stream containing fine sand indicates erosion even before a storm.

C is incorrect because the appearance of coarse sand and pebbles in the sediment indicate a higher rate of erosion after a storm.

D is correct because the particle load, or size of particles, is greater after a storm, and large par-ticles cause more erosion than small particles.

5. C

A is incorrect because an alluvial fan forms because of a change in slope and speed, not from an increase in water volume.

B is incorrect because sediment falls out because the land is flatter, not because the land is steeper.

C is correct because as the stream entered an area with a lower slope, it spread out and moved slower, and the slower speed caused sediment to drop out.

D is incorrect because an alluvial fan forms as a stream spreads out and becomes wider.

Lesson 4 Quiz

1. D   4. B
2. A   5. B
3. B

1. D

A is incorrect because a dune is an example of deposition by wind, not mass movement caused by gravity.

B is incorrect because loess is an example of deposition by wind, not mass movement caused by gravity.

C is incorrect because a glacier is an example of erosion and deposition by ice, not mass move-ment caused by gravity.

D is correct because a mudslide is an example of mass movement caused by gravity.

2. A

A is correct because loess is rich in minerals and forms good soil for growing crops.

B is incorrect because loess does not contain bits of rock; it is made of layers of fine-grained sediment.

C is incorrect because loess does erode easily, which is not a property that makes it valuable.

D is incorrect because loess is not difficult to find.

3. B

A is incorrect because the sediment does not play a role in whether the lake will dry up; the sediment is necessary to form a shoreline to contain the water.

B is correct because without the sediment, the water would not stay contained.

C is incorrect because although vegetation needs sediment in order to grow, vegetation is not necessary for the formation of the lake.

D is incorrect because sediment does not play a role in ice melting.

4. B

A is incorrect because although it must be below freezing for a glacier to form, there must also be lots of snow, so it will not usually be dry.

B is correct because for a glacier to form it must be cold and more snow must fall than melts, so the snow can be compacted into a glacier.

C is incorrect because although there must be a fair amount of precipitation, it must be cold, not mild, for a glacier to form.

D is incorrect because although it must be below freezing for a glacier to form, more snow must fall than melts.

5. B

A is incorrect because the lake bed was dry, so ice was not a factor in forming the dunes; rather, the sand was blown from the lake bed by wind.

B is correct because wind is the agent responsible for the formation of the sand dunes, with the sand at the bottom of the dry lake bed.

C is incorrect because the lake bed was dry, so water could not have formed the dunes.

D is incorrect because gravity would pull sediment and sand toward Earth, and because the sand dunes rise above the lake bed, they were most likely formed by wind.

Lesson 5 Quiz

1. A   4. A
2. C   5. C
3. D

1. A

A is correct because soil formation begins with rock breaking up into small pieces.

B is incorrect because bedrock is solid rock that lies below layers of soil.

C is incorrect because ice wedging involves water freezing and thawing in cracks of rock.

D is incorrect because rock is an inorganic material. Organic material is made of once-living material.

2. C

A is incorrect because the water that seeps into the soil will cause chemical weathering.

B is incorrect because erosion does not aid in soil formation.

C is correct because the mixing action of larger burrowing animals helps the function of de-composers and the aeration of the soil.

D is incorrect because exfoliation is not the process by which the tortoise breaks up rocks.

3. D

A is incorrect because although larger animals can affect the physical characteristics of soil by digging burrows, microorganisms are too small to dig burrows.

B is incorrect because atmospheric forces, not microorganisms, are the agents of weathering on Earth's surface.

C is incorrect because pore spaces and moisture describe physical characteristics of soil; also, microorganisms are too small to have much effect on the presence of pore spaces in soil.

D is correct because microorganisms decompose dead organisms and return nutrients to the soil, which affects the soil's chemistry.

4. A

A is correct because the organic and chemical nutrients that plants need to grow are most abun-dant in horizon A

B is incorrect because rock fragments have little to do with soil fertility.

C is incorrect because soil fertility is the soil's ability to hold and supply nutrients to plants, not the ability to hold or supply water.

D is incorrect because the solid rock in horizon D contains little organic material, so does not contribute to soil fertility.

5. C

A is incorrect because pore spaces are spaces between soil particles through which water and air can move.

B is incorrect because humus is dark, organic material, whereas weathered sediment is inorganic material.

C is correct because humus is dark, organic material formed in soil from the decayed remains of plants and animals.

D is incorrect because soil is a loose mixture of rock fragments, organic material, water, and air that can support the growth of vegetation.

Lesson 1 Alternative Assessment

What's in a Sphere?: Poems include five stanzas, each of which discusses a one of Earth's spheres.

Advertising Earth: Brochures include information about the Earth system and the ways Earth's spheres work together. They also include an illustration of Earth.

Peeling Back the Layers: PowerPoint presentations include information about each of Earth's layers. They also include an illustration that depicts the layers.

Earth's Story: Stories are written from Earth's point of view. In the stories, Earth discusses its spheres and gives at least three ways the spheres interact.

Fan Club: Web sites include information about the astrosphere's composition and size. They also include ways the atmosphere makes life on Earth safer.

Biosphere Breakdown: The acrostic is complete and the topics students use are appropriate and relevant to the biosphere.

Where's the Water? Posters accurately depict the hydrosphere, and the different parts of the hydrosphere are labeled.

Composing Questions: Worksheets include at least five questions or activities dealing with the cryosphere.

Lesson 2 Alternative Assessment

Crossword Puzzle: Puzzles include different agents of weathering. Puzzles use definitions and descriptions of the specific types of weathering caused by the agent.

Illustration of Agents: Illustration includes several agents of weathering, either physical or chemical, such as wind, rain, sun, ice, water, gravity, plant and animals' actions, acid precipitation,

oxygen in air, acids in living things, and acids in water.

Wanted Poster: Poster includes pictures and descriptions about how each agent causes chemical weathering.

Model: Model shows an area that has experienced at least two kinds of chemical weathering. Model includes labeled descriptions on how the weathering occurred.

Quiz: Quiz questions ask about agents of physical weathering, how physical weathering occurs, and what the results of physical weathering are. Answers to questions are be included.

Newspaper Article: Article describes a newsworthy example of chemical weathering, and describes other types of weathering as background information for the reader.

Interview with a Landform: Interviewed questions and answers describe weathering from the past, and what it expects in the future. A picture showing the weathering is included.

Timeline: Timeline describes the sequence of physical and chemical weathering that has occurred to a material. Pictures show what the material looks like at different points along the timeline.

Lesson 3 Alternative Assessment

Photograph of a landform: Each erosion and deposition process is correctly identified and described.

Observations of a stream: Each example of surface stream processes is explained correctly (role of gravity, gradient, discharge, particle load, particle size and how each relate to the rate of erosion and deposition).

Observations of a coast: How the land was eroded or formed by waves/currents is correctly explained.

An aerial photograph of an alluvial fan: Description of alluvial fan, its characteristics, and actions that caused its formation are correctly explained.

Observations of a local farm: Each erosion and deposition process is correctly identified and described.

Website describing national parks: Each erosion and deposition process is correctly identified and described.

Descriptions or photographs of a flood: The flood, its characteristics, and the erosion and deposition it causes are described correctly.

Topographical map: The land, its characteristics, and the action that caused its formation are described correctly.

Descriptions or photographs of a coastline before and after a big storm: Description of how the land was eroded or formed by water and waves is correct.

Geological map: Description of the land, its characteristics, and what action caused its formation is correct.

Lesson 4 Alternative Assessment

Desert Pavement: Answers describe characteristics of desert pavement, and why it looks the way it does.

Dunes: Answers explain characteristics of dunes and why they do not stay the same over time.

Loess: Answers describe deposition that occurs to make loess so fertile.

Alpine Glacier: Answers describe the features alpine glaciers can make, and how this occurs.

Continental Glacier: Answers describe how big a continental glacier can be, where you find continental glaciers, and how a continental glacier is different from an alpine glacier.

Glacial Drift: Answers describe how glacial drift material was deposited.

Creep: Answers describe the characteristics of creep.

Rock Fall and Landslides: Answers describe the conditions that create rock falls and landslides.

Mudflows and Lahars: Answers explain why a mudflow is dangerous, where a mudflow can occur, and the difference between a mudflow and a lahar.

Lesson 5 Alternative Assessment

Realistic illustration: Student illustrations should show the important features of their chosen soil topics.

Schematic diagram with a key: Students should create a scientific diagram that uses symbols to provide data about soil in a certain area.

Model: Student models should clearly and accurately display their chosen topics about soil.

Informational booklet, such as a field guide: Student booklets should creatively present information about soil. For example, a student might write a field guide giving a detailed description of the soil characteristics of a specific location.

Multimedia presentation: Student should design a website or build a digital slideshow to present information about their soil topics.

Student choice: Student should use an appropriate mode of presenting relevant information about their soil topics.

Performance-Based Assessment

See Unit 1, Lesson 2

1. Answers will vary. Sample answer: The wood is yellow with a dark brown knot. The surface is flat and smooth except for the knot, which is rough and grainy with varying coloration patterns.

4. The surface of the plain wood and the knotty wood are both worn down. However, the plain wood is more worn down than the knotty wood.

5. The sand paper wears down, or abrades, the wood much like mechanical forces erode rocks on Earth's surfaces.

6. Both the wood and the sandpaper are worn down in this activity. They both became smoother when they

were rubbed against each other.

7. Answers will vary. Sample answers: I could use an eye dropper to drop an acidic liquid on the wood. One limitation would be that it would take a very long time to see results.

Unit Review

Vocabulary

1. **humus** See Unit 1, Lesson 5

2. **chemical weathering** See Unit 1, Lesson 2

3. **delta** See Unit 1, Lesson 3

4. **glacial drift** See Unit 1, Lesson 4

5. **biosphere** See Unit 1, Lesson 1

Key Concepts

6. B   9. C   12. B
7. B   10. A
8. D   11. C

6. B See Unit 1, Lesson 5

A is incorrect because soil chemistry is a measure of the pH and chemical makeup of the soil.

B is correct because soil fertility is the ability of the soil to support plant growth.

C is incorrect because texture describes the size of the soil particles.

D is incorrect because pore space describes the spaces between the soil particles.

7. B See Unit 1, Lesson 2

A is incorrect because sunlight does not directly break down rock and glacial melting does

not break down rocks, it deposits sediment.

B is correct because rocks are broken down by chemical and physical weathering, such as dissolution and freeze-thaw.

C is incorrect because deposition is a process in which sediments and materials are accumulated in a certain area.

D is incorrect because humus does not break down rock.

8. D See Unit 1, Lesson 3

A is incorrect because this describes a delta, not an alluvial fan.

B is incorrect because this describes a floodplain, not an alluvial fan.

C is incorrect because this describes an oxbow lake, not an alluvial fan.

D is correct because an alluvial fan is a fan-shaped deposit of sediment that is formed over time as a stream deposits its load. Typically, this is due to the stream slowing down when entering a flat area of land.

9. C See Unit 1, Lesson 3

A is incorrect because rough waves would erode the smaller sediments away, leaving larger sediments.

B is incorrect because rough waves would erode any sandbars that formed.

C is correct because stormy seas and rough waves would erode all of the smaller sediment leaving larger

sediments such as pebbles and rocks.

D is incorrect because sea stacks are offshore formations and Antonio is observing the shore.

10. A See Unit 1, Lesson 4

A is correct because gravity is a cause of landslides, rockfalls, and creep.

B is incorrect because sunlight (solar energy) does not cause landslides, rockfalls, or creep.

C is incorrect because oxidation causes chemical weathering, but does not directly cause land-slides, rockfalls, or creep.

D is incorrect because wind erosion does not directly cause landslides, rockfalls, or creep.

11. C See Unit 1, Lesson 3

A is incorrect because it describes a cavern, which has a roof.

B is incorrect because it describes surface erosion by a mountainous stream, which does not cause sinkholes to form.

C is correct because a sinkhole forms when the roof of a cavern collapses and results in a formation like what is shown in the diagram.

D is incorrect because it is describing surface erosion and channel formation, caused by a stream eroding sediments along its path.

12. B See Unit 1, Lesson 4

A   is incorrect because it does not need to be very dry to form glaciers.

B   is correct because for a glacier to form the temperature must be below freezing and more snow must fall than melts, so the snow can be compacted into a glacier.

C   is incorrect because although there must be a fair amount of precipitation, it must be in the form of snow.

D   is incorrect because more snow must fall than melt.

Critical Thinking
13. See Unit 1, Lesson 2

• Water is a cause of both physical and chemical weathering.

• Water can cause physical weathering by causing abrasion, in which rocks bump into each other and break down into smaller pieces. Water causes physical weathering in other ways as well.

• Water can cause chemical weathering by dissolving certain minerals in the rocks.

14. See Unit 1, Lesson 5

• The A horizon is the top layer of soil. It contains the most humus, which gives it a dark color. Actions by plants and animals affect this horizon the most.

• The B horizon is below the A horizon. Materials from the A horizon move down to the B horizon through the process of leaching. The B horizon contains less organic matter than the overlying A horizon.

• The C horizon is below the B horizon. It is partially weathered parent rock. It contains little to no decayed organic matter and typically has larger particles than the horizons above.

Connect Essential Questions
15. See Unit 1, Lesson 3 and Lesson 4

A. Gravity works with water by causing it to move downward, which causes erosion in many cases. One example is a stream. The stream flows because of gravity. The flow causes erosion of material in its path. Gravity causes glaciers to move down-slope, and glaciers erode rock underneath of them.

B. Water erodes and transports these materials and eventually deposits them. A stream can carry a sediment load, and when it slows down, some sediment is deposited (for example a delta or an alluvial fan). When a glacier melts, the sediment it has eroded and picked up from before is deposited (for example, a glacial moraine).

Unit Test A
Key Concepts

1.	A	5.	A	9.	D
2.	A	6.	D	10.	B
3.	C	7.	B	11.	C
4.	D	8.	C	12.	B

1. A

A   is correct because river water slows as it enters the ocean,

causing sand to be deposited and a delta to be formed.

B   is incorrect because sand is not deposited because of a mixing of the two water types.

C   is incorrect because sand deposited at a delta comes from the river water, not from sand transported by waves.

D   is incorrect because sand deposited at a delta comes from slowing river water, not from slow-ing ocean water.

2. A

A   is correct because rain causes chemical weathering, and wind causes physical weathering.

B   is incorrect because the deposition of sand on top of the granite would help protect the granite from weathering agents.

C   is incorrect because weathering does not happen to rocks deep within the ground.

D   is incorrect because underground pressure helps form rocks, not weather them.

3. C

A   is incorrect because precipitation in Texas has the highest pH (lowest acidity), so rocks there will break down more slowly from acid precipitation than in other states.

B   is incorrect because precipitation in California has the second highest pH (second lowest acidity), so rocks there will break down more slowly from acid precipitation than in all other states except for Texas.

C is correct because precipitation in New York has the lowest pH (highest acidity), so rocks there will break down more quickly from acid precipitation than in the other states.

D is incorrect because precipitation in Washington has the second lowest pH (second highest acidity), so rocks there will break down more slowly from acid precipitation than in New York.

4. D

A is incorrect because valleys generally form because of erosion by surface water, not ground-water.

B is incorrect because canyons generally form because of erosion by surface water, not groundwater.

C is incorrect because human-made channels do not form because of erosion.

D is correct because caverns form when groundwater dissolves and erodes rock underground.

5. A

A is correct because the speed of water flow increases with an increase in slope, and a faster flow of water causes more erosion than a slower flow of water.

B is incorrect because the speed of the water and the amount

of erosion would both increase with an increased slope.

C is incorrect because the amount of erosion would increase with an increased slope.

D is incorrect because the speed of the water would increase with an increased slope.

6. D

A is incorrect because humus is found mostly in horizon A, not in bedrock.

B is incorrect because horizon B contains little organic matter.

C is incorrect because parent rock is another name for bedrock.

D is correct because humus is organic matter made of decayed plants and animals.

7. B

A is incorrect because reactions with air that cause color changes are chemical changes.

B is correct because wind causes abrasion, which can change the shape of rocks.

C is incorrect because reactions with water are chemical changes, not physical changes (abrasion).

D is incorrect because a layer falling off because of a reduction in pressure is exfoliation, not abrasion.

8. C

A is incorrect because the atmosphere is composed of 78% nitrogen, 21% oxygen, and 1% other gases.

B is incorrect because the atmosphere is composed of 78% nitrogen, 21% oxygen, and 1% other gases.

C is correct because the atmosphere is composed of 78% nitrogen, 21% oxygen, and 1% other gases.

D is incorrect because the atmosphere is composed of 78% nitrogen, 21% oxygen, and 1% other gases.

9. D

A is incorrect because when the wind slows, it will drop the heaviest sediment first, and the biggest sediment may not be the heaviest sediment.

B is incorrect because the wind will drop the heaviest sediment first, not the lightest.

C is incorrect because the wind will drop the heaviest sediment first, not the smallest.

D is correct because when the wind slows, it will drop the heaviest sediment first.

10. B

A is incorrect because the crust is located farther from the core than the mantle is.

B is correct because the core is the innermost layer, the mantle is located outside of the core, and the crust is located outside of the mantle.

C is incorrect because the mantle is located outside of the core. The atmosphere is a separate sphere.

D is incorrect because the atmosphere is not part of the

geosphere, the crust is the outermost layer of the geosphere, and the mantle is located below the crust.

11. C

A is incorrect because gravity, not ice, is the force responsible for landslides, mudslides, and rockfalls.

B is incorrect because gravity, not wind, is the force responsible for landslides, mudslides, and rockfalls.

C is correct because gravity is the force responsible for landslides, mudslides, and rockfalls.

D is incorrect because gravity, not temperature, is the force responsible for landslides, mud-slides, and rockfalls.

12. B

A is incorrect because the thickness of the humus layer depends on many factors, not just the composition of the parent rock.

B is correct because the composition of soil is strongly influenced by the parent rock.

C is incorrect because the thickness of a soil horizon depends on climate, topography, and time much more than on the composition of the parent rock.

D is incorrect because the amount of organic matter depends on the climate and the number and types of living things in the area, not the composition of the parent rock.

Critical Thinking
13.

- a U-shaped profile (e.g., *After the glacier moves through this valley, it should look U-shaped;* etc.)

- an explanation that glaciers cause erosion and the breaking up of rock and carry the rock and sediment, pushing it to the sides to create a U-shaped valley from a V-shaped valley (e.g., *The glacier will cause erosion and break up rock in the valley. Then it will carry the rock and sediment and push it to the sides, creating a U-shaped valley;* etc.)

Extended Response
14.

- hydrosphere, as liquid water in oceans, rivers, lakes, or groundwater (e.g., *The hydrosphere stores liquid water in the oceans;* etc.)

- cryosphere, as solid water (ice) (e.g., *The cryosphere stores ice in the polar icecaps;* etc.)

- atmosphere, as water vapor or precipitation (e.g., *The atmosphere stores water vapor that comes from evaporation of ocean water;* etc.)

- biosphere, as liquid water in organisms (e.g., *The biosphere stores liquid water in the bodies of plants and animals;* etc.)

- geosphere, as liquid water in aquifers (e.g., *The geosphere stores liquid water as groundwater;* etc.)

Unit Test B
Key Concepts

1.	A	5.	B	9.	A
2.	D	6.	A	10.	A
3.	D	7.	A	11.	B
4.	A	8.	C	12.	B

1. A

A is correct because a delta forms as a river enters an ocean or sea.

B is incorrect because a delta forms when a river enters an ocean or sea and cannot form in mountains.

C is incorrect because an alluvial fan could be formed at this point, but a delta could not be formed.

D is incorrect because a delta forms when a river enters an ocean or sea and cannot form on a plain.

2. D

A is incorrect because weathering does not happen to rocks deep within the ground.

B is incorrect because granite is too hard for organisms to burrow into.

C is incorrect because underground pressure helps form rocks, not weather them.

D is correct because plant acids act to chemically break down the minerals that comprise granite.

3. D

A is incorrect because both locations have acidic precipitation, which is an agent of chemical weathering.

B is incorrect because the acidity of the precipitation in New York is greater than in Washington, so it will break down rocks faster.

C is incorrect because the acidity of the precipitation in New York is greater than in Washington, so it will break down rocks faster.

D is correct because the acidity of the precipitation in New York is greater than in Washington, so it will break down rocks faster.

4. A

A is correct because caverns form when groundwater dissolves and erodes rock underground.

B is incorrect because the stream described in this statement is an example of the formation of landforms by stream erosion.

C is incorrect because the sea cave described in this statement is an example of the formation of landforms by waves.

D is incorrect because the delta described in this statement is an example of the formation of landforms by stream deposition.

5. B

A is incorrect because the bucket of water is greater for the bucket of water, and a greater amount of water causes more erosion to happen.

B is correct because the amount of water is greater for the

bucket of water, and a greater amount of water causes more erosion to happen.

C is incorrect because the cup of water and the bucket of water would both cause erosion.

D is incorrect because the bucket of water is greater for the bucket of water, and a greater amount of water causes more erosion to happen.

6. A

A is correct because humus is found mostly in the A horizon, the topmost layer.

B is incorrect because the B horizon contains relatively little organic matter.

C is incorrect because the C horizon contains relatively little organic matter.

D is incorrect because horizon D is composed of bedrock.

7. A

A is correct because abrasion removes parts of a rock, making it smaller.

B is incorrect because the deposition of sediment is not a direct result of abrasion.

C is incorrect because changes in the surface color of a rock are caused by chemical weathering, not abrasion.

D is incorrect because abrasion is the wearing away of a rock's surface, not the transportation of the rock to a new location.

8. C

A is incorrect because the atmosphere is composed of 78% nitrogen, 21% oxygen, and 1% other gases.

B is incorrect because the atmosphere is composed of 78% nitrogen, 21% oxygen, and 1% other gases.

C is correct because the atmosphere is composed of 78% nitrogen, 21% oxygen, and 1% other gases.

D is incorrect because the atmosphere is composed of 78% nitrogen, 21% oxygen, and 1% other gases.

9. A

A is correct because dunes are formed by the transport and deposition of sediment by wind.

B is incorrect because dunes, not glaciers, are formed by the transport and deposition of sediment by wind. Glaciers form in cold areas where snow builds up and turns into ice.

C is incorrect because dunes, not rockfalls, are formed by the transport and deposition of sediment by wind. In rockfalls, blocks of rock drop freely down cliffs or mountainsides.

D is incorrect because dunes, not mudflows, are formed by the transport and deposition of sediment by wind. Mudflows move like a liquid.

10. A

A is correct because the crust is the outermost layer, the

mantle is located below the crust, and the core is the innermost part of the geosphere and is surrounded by the mantle.

B is incorrect because the core is the innermost part of the geosphere, and is surrounded by the mantle, which is in turn surrounded by the crust.

C is incorrect because the atmosphere is not considered to be a part of the geosphere; the outermost part of the geosphere is the crust.

D is incorrect because the atmosphere is not considered to be a part of the geosphere; the in-nermost part of the geosphere is the core.

11. B

A is incorrect because rain, not ice, is the most likely condition that triggers mudslides.

B is correct because rain is the most likely condition that triggers mudslides.

C is incorrect because rain, not wind, is the most likely condition that triggers mudslides.

D is incorrect because rain, not temperature, is the most likely condition that triggers mudslides.

12. B

A is incorrect because a thick layer of humus can develop only after the rock has broken down to the point that C and B horizons develop.

B is correct because the rock must first be broken down

physically and chemically in order for soil to start forming.

C is incorrect because the transportation of pieces of the granite to other locations does not be-gin the process of soil formation in the area where the granite is exposed on Earth's surface.

D is incorrect because the decomposition of organic matter contributes to the development of the A horizon, not to the beginning of soil formation from parent rock.

Critical Thinking
13.

• a drawing of a valley with a U-shaped profile. *Please see example of drawing in the Visual Answers section at the end of this Answer Key.*

• an explanation that the drawing shows that the glacier changed the V-shaped valley shown to a U-shaped valley because glaciers erode and break up the rock that makes up the side of a V-shaped valley (e.g., *The glacier eroded the rock that made up the sides of the valley, causing it to change into a U-shaped valley; etc.*)

Extended Response
14.

two of the following:

• cryosphere: freezing or melting (e.g., *Water can move between the hydrosphere and cryosphere by melting or freezing; etc*)

• atmosphere: evaporation or condensation and then

precipitation (e.g., *Water can move between the hydrosphere and the atmosphere by evaporation or precipitation; etc.*)

• biosphere: consumption, elimination, respiration, transpiration, or decomposition (e.g., *Water can move between the hydrosphere and the biosphere when animals drink water;* etc.)

• geosphere: infiltration from runoff, outflow from wells or springs (e.g., *Water can move between the geosphere and the hydrosphere when people pump groundwater out of a well;* etc.)

Unit 2 Earth's History
Unit Pretest

1. C   5. B   9. D
2. C   6. B   10. D
3. B   7. A
4. C   8. B

1. C

A is incorrect because floods are short-term events, not slow, gradual processes that occur over long periods of time.

B is incorrect because droughts are short-term events, not slow, gradual processes that occur over long periods of time.

C is correct because, according to the principle of uniformitarianism, geologic processes occur in a regular fashion over long periods of time.

D is incorrect because floods are short-term events, not

slow, gradual processes that occur over long periods of time.

2. C

A is incorrect because index fossils have not been found in samples of rock from elsewhere in the solar system.

B is incorrect because radiocarbon dating has a useful time range of up to about 45,000 years old, and can only be used to date organic materials.

C is correct because uranium-lead dating has a useful time range for rock samples from else-where in the solar system.

D is incorrect because sedimentary rocks contain many different minerals with various parent isotopes and cannot be directly dated.

3. B

A is incorrect because the rarity of the isotopes is not the reason they can be used to date rocks.

B is correct because these isotopes decay at set rates, so they can be used to date rocks.

C is incorrect because the size of the isotopes is not the reason they can be used to date rocks.

D is incorrect because the isotopes are not stable over time; they decay because they are unstable.

4. C

A is incorrect because the black boxes show that the drilling took place in the Pacific Ocean.

B is incorrect because there is no need to drill into the Earth to study surface landforms.

C is correct because the drilling took place in the Pacific Ocean.

D is incorrect because amber forms as tree sap hardens, and that does not happen in a marine environment.

5. B

A is incorrect because the type of rock is the main reason the granite is easier to date than the sandstone.

B is correct. Igneous rocks are a very good type of rock to use for dating because of how the minerals in the rock form.

C is incorrect because the type of rock is the main reason the granite is easier to date than the sandstone.

D is incorrect because granite is igneous, not sedimentary.

6. B

A is incorrect because volcanic eruptions may occur as tectonic plates move apart, but they do not cause tectonic plates to move.

B is correct because the continents have been moving throughout Earth's history as a result of tectonic plate movement.

C is incorrect because weathering and erosion can break down Earth's surface features, but do not cause continents to move.

D is incorrect because the movement of continents is a result of tectonic plate

movement, which is not cyclical.

7. A

A is correct because the end of the Mesozoic Era is defined by the mass extinction event that eliminated the dinosaurs.

B is incorrect because dinosaurs did not evolve until much later, in the Mesozoic Era.

C is incorrect because dinosaurs had not yet evolved at the beginning of the Mesozoic Era.

D is incorrect because dinosaurs did not evolve until much later, in the Mesozoic Era.

8. B

A is incorrect because the principle of superposition is based on the layering of rocks, not proximity.

B is correct because the law of superposition states that an undisturbed sedimentary rock layer is older than the layers above it and younger than the layers below it.

C is incorrect because the principle of superposition is based on the layering of rocks.

D is incorrect because the law of superposition uses rock layers in their original positions to determine their relative ages, not their exact ages.

9. D

A is incorrect because fossil G did not appear until a later period, so fossil F and fossil G cannot be in the same rock layer.

B is incorrect because fossil F appeared only in period 3, so the rock layer must have been made dur-ing that period only.

C is incorrect because fossil H appeared in an older period than did fossil F.

D is correct because a rock layer that contains fossil F was formed in period 3, a more recent period than period 4.

10. D

A is incorrect. The law of crosscutting relationships is one way to determine the relative age of rocks because any rock that cuts through other rock is younger than the rock being cut through.

B is incorrect because a principle of geology states that rocks that cut through other rocks are younger than the rocks being cut.

C is incorrect because the fault is younger than the rocks it cuts through.

D is correct because the law of crosscutting relationships states that a fault is younger than any other body of rock that it cuts through.

Lesson 1 Quiz

1. A   4. A
2. B   5. D
3. C

1. A

A is correct because water gradually eroded the rock to form an arch.

B is incorrect because abrasion is the wearing away of rock through the mechanical action of other rocks or sand particles.

C is incorrect because volcanism is the process of transferring magma and hot, molten material from Earth's interior to its surface. The figure shows how water can erode rock.

D is incorrect because deposition is the process by which new materials are laid down, or deposited.

2. B

A is incorrect because deposition is the process by which materials are laid down.

B is correct because weathering and erosion wear away rocks and remove material to make them smaller and smoother.

C is incorrect because the movement of continents does not cause mountain ranges to become lower or more rounded over time.

D is incorrect because collisions between continental plates would most likely cause mountain ranges to form, rather than becoming lower and more rounded.

3. C

A is incorrect because radiometric dating shows that Earth is about 4.6 billion years old, not 40 billion years old.

B is incorrect because based on radiometric dating of rock from our solar system, Earth is about 4.6 billion years old.

C is correct because radiometric dating of rock from our solar system indicates that Earth is about 4.6 billion years.

D is incorrect because Earth is about 4.6 billion, not 4.6 million, years old.

4. A

A is correct because the concentration of gases in ice indicates the conditions of the atmosphere at the time the ice was formed.

B is incorrect because ice cores provide information about climate conditions in the past and not about the movement of continents.

C is incorrect because ice core samples do not contain a fossil record that shows the evolution of a new species.

D is incorrect because the ice core samples are taken deep from beneath the Earth's surface.

5. D

A is incorrect because trace fossils take as much time to form as do body fossils.

B is incorrect because body fossils can form in ice, asphalt, and amber.

C is incorrect because most marine organisms do not live on soft sediment.

D is correct because an animal has only one body, but it can produce many imprints over its lifetime.

Lesson 2 Quiz

1. B   4. C
2. B   5. D
3. B

1. B

A is incorrect because determining mineral

composition is not part of relative dating, which is used to compare the ages of rocks.

B   is correct because relative dating is used to determine the order in which rock layers formed and the relative age of each rock layer.

C   is incorrect because classifying rocks by their type is not a way to determine which rock is older than another rock.

D   is incorrect because radioactive isotopes are used to determine the absolute age, not the relative age, of rocks.

2.   B

A   is incorrect because the fault cuts through all of the layers, rock 1 cuts through rock 2, and rock 2 cuts through layer 1.

B   is correct because layer 1 is cut by both rock bodies and the fault. Therefore, layer 1 is the oldest. The fault is the youngest because it cuts through all the other features. Rock 1 cuts through, and is younger than, rock 2.

C   is incorrect because the fault cuts through all of the layers, rock 1 cuts through rock 2, and rock 2 cuts through layer 1.

D   is incorrect because the fault cuts through all of the layers, rock 1 cuts through rock 2, and rock 2 cuts through layer 1.

3.   B

A   is incorrect because many animals that exist today have not existed throughout Earth's history.

B   is correct because animals that live on Earth today have descended from animals that existed in the past.

C   is incorrect because animals today have descended from animals that once existed, so fossil and modern animals share many characteristics.

D   is incorrect because animals that lived in the past may or may not be more complex than those living today.

4.   C

A   is incorrect because minerals are not used to determine the relative ages of rocks.

B   is incorrect because the geologist determined the relative ages, not the absolute ages.

C   is correct because the law states that an undisturbed sedimentary rock layer is older than the layers above it and younger than the layers below it.

D   is incorrect because an unconformity takes place when there is a break in the geologic record.

5.   D

A   is incorrect because a geologic column refers to an arrangement of rocks that is based on the relative ages of the rocks.

B   is incorrect because a body of rock that cuts through sedimentary rock is called an intrusion, not a geologic column.

C   is incorrect because any rock removed from the ground to study is called a sample.

D   is correct because a geologic column is an ordered arrangement of rock layers that is based on the relative ages of the rocks, in which the oldest rocks are at the bottom.

Lesson 3 Quiz

1. C   4. A
2. C   5. C
3. B

1.   C

A   is incorrect because lead-208 is the daughter isotope.

B   is incorrect because thorium-232 is the parent isotope.

C   is correct because thorium-232 (parent) is shown decaying to form lead-208 (daughter).

D   is incorrect because thorium-232 is the parent isotope, and lead-208 is the daughter isotope.

2.   C

A   is incorrect because Earth formed 4.6 billion years ago, not 3.5 million years ago.

B   is incorrect because Earth formed 4.6 billion years ago, not 700 million years ago.

C   is correct because the approximate age of Earth has been determined to be 4.6 billion years.

D   is incorrect because Earth formed 4.6 billion years ago, not 12 billion years ago.

3. B

A   is incorrect because it is a definition of relative dating.

B   is correct because *absolute dating* is defined as "any method of measuring the age of an event or object in years."

C   is incorrect because it describes radiometric dating, which is only one method of absolute dating.

D   is incorrect because the use of index fossils is only one method of absolute dating.

4. A

A   is correct because the age of the mineral in years can be found by multiplying the length of the half-life in years by the number of half-lives potassium-40 has decayed.

B   is incorrect because the amount of energy released is not needed to determine the age of the mineral.

C   is incorrect because the mass of a potassium atom is not needed to determine the age of the rock sample.

D   is incorrect because argon-40 does not decay into any other material.

5. C

A   is incorrect because distinctiveness is a key characteristic of index fossils.

B   is incorrect because it is not a key characteristic of index fossils.

C   is correct because a short span of existence is a key characteristic of index fossils.

D   is incorrect because abundance is a key characteristic of index fossils.

Lesson 4 Quiz

1. A   4. A
2. C   5. A
3. C

1. A

A   is correct because eras are subdivided into periods.

B   is incorrect because epochs are a subdivision of both eras and periods.

C   is incorrect because eons are longer spans of time than eras are.

D   is incorrect because both eras and periods have boundaries that are marked by mass extinction events.

2. C

A   is incorrect because the Cretaceous, Jurassic, and Triassic are all periods, not eras.

B   is incorrect because the Paleocene, Eocene, and Oligocene are all epochs, not eras.

C   is correct because the three eras are the Paleozoic, Cenozoic, and Mesozoic.

D   is incorrect because Precambrian time is the span of time before eras, and the Cambrian and Devonian are both periods, not eras.

3. C

A   is incorrect because Earth's major structural layers formed early in Earth's history.

B   is incorrect because many of the changes in the solar system have not impacted Earth's history as recorded in its rocks.

C   is correct because major divisions of the geologic time scale are chosen to mark major events, such as mass extinctions, that occurred in the history of life.

D   is incorrect because the movement of continents is a slow, gradual process that has no distinct endpoints.

4. A

A   is correct because geology is the study of Earth's past and all of the processes that shape Earth.

B   is incorrect because the study of the history of the solar system belongs mainly to the fields of planetary geology and astronomy.

C   is incorrect because the study of living things and their evolution belong mainly to the field of biology.

D   is incorrect because the study of Earth's atmosphere belongs mainly to the field of meteorology.

5. A

A   is correct because the collision of continental landmasses such as Africa and North America caused the crust to fold and thicken, forming the Appalachian Mountains.

B   is incorrect because the Appalachian Mountains are not volcanic in origin.

C is incorrect because the Appalachian Mountains ceased forming as the continents split apart.

D is incorrect because the Appalachian Mountains formed from the collision of continents, not from the energy released by seismic activity.

Lesson 1 Alternative Assessment

Fossil Club: Web sites summarize the ways fossils form, and includes one picture of each type of fossil.

Club Headquarters: Posters describe how sedimentary rock can give scientists information about Earth's past, and include two images of sedimentary rocks.

Climate Quiz: Quizzes contain at least five questions that deal with Earth's climate and the changes it has undergone.

Climate Clues: News reports describe the fossil findings and tells what the plant evidence indicates about the climate in the past.

The Aging Earth: Speeches define uniformitarianism, and explain how it helps to determine Earth's age.

Move Along: Scripts define plate tectonics and the evidence that supports it.

Lesson 2 Alternative Assessment

Sedimentary Summary: Pamphlets describe sedimentary rock formation and include two illustra-tions of undisturbed sedimentary rock layers.

This Just In!: New reports identify a section of disturbed of sedimentary rock and talk about how the rock was disturbed. Reports also discuss ways scientists can correctly date the disturbed rock.

Relative Dating: Poems, reports, or Websites include illustrations and defines and describes relative dating, and explains the methods scientists use to conduct relative dating.

Functional Fossils: Models show a plant or animal fossil, describe what the fossil might tell about the age of the rock in which it was found, and how scientists use fossils to determine relative ages.

A Scientist's Story: Stories include a scientist who is dating sedimentary rocks. Stories also explain the law of superposition and how it helps date the rocks.

Explaining Geologic Columns: Speeches explain the ideas behind geologic columns, how scientists collect information about geologic columns, and how scientists use geologic columns.

Important Principles: Diagrams or models show the island's geologic column, and explain the rela-tive ages of rock layers.

Understanding Unconformities: Posters show and describe ways layers can be changed or dis-turbed, and include labels.

Lesson 3 Alternative Assessment

Half-Life Breakdown: Displays explain what a half-life is, and discuss how scientists use half-life in radiometric dating.

You Ask the Questions: Quizzes contain at least four questions that deal with index fossils and the ways scientists use them.

Which Is Best?: Memos explain which sample to use and why.

Decay Drama: Skits explain how radioactive decay makes it possible for scientists to date objects.

Dating Description: Presentations list and describe the different methods of radiometric dating. They include information about the best situations in which to use each method.

Absolute Persuasion: Speeches explain what absolute dating is, and why the exhibit is needed.

Meeting the Requirements: Web pages explain the requirements fossils must meet to be considered index fossils.

Come on Down!: Press releases explain what absolute dating is and why people should visit the ex-hibit.

How Old Is Earth?: Songs describe how scientists determine Earth's age.

Lesson 4 Alternative Assessment

Big Change Coming: Pictures show a volcanic eruption, earthquake, tsunami, meteor collision, or any natural event that could cause sudden change to Earth's surface.

Name Game: Presentations explain that there is no agreed-upon system for naming geologic periods. Many periods are named for the area in which rocks of a certain age were first found or studied.

Earth Diary: Diaries include facts about the climate conditions and geologic events in each era of the Phanerozoic eon.

Interview from the Past: Interviews present Hutton's views on uniformitarianism, and explain how these views differ from catastrophism and modern views.

Lights Out: A sample model might involve placing two plants under a lamp. A cloth would be placed over one of the plants to model the debris that enters the sky following a volcanic eruption.

On the Move: Models show an accurate representation of Earth's continents. Students are able to use the model to show how the continents have moved at several significant points in Earth's history, in-cluding the end of the Precambrian time, the Paleozoic Era, the Mesozoic Era, and the Cenozoic Era.

Geologic Time Puzzle: Puzzles include distinctive clues for each time division.

Performance-Based Assessment

See Unit 2, Lesson 1

2. The first year of the tree's life should be indicated by a leader line pointing to the very center of the cross section; a year of higher than normal rainfall should be indicated by a leader line pointing to any ring that is very wide in comparison to the others; a two-year period of drought should be indicated by a leader line pointing to two rings that are much narrower than other rings; evidence of a forest fire should be indicated by a leader line pointing to the blackened section of the rings in the lower left center of the cross section.

3. Sample answer: This example of a tree ring shows a pattern of changing ring size that matches changes in local rainfall over several years. This way of "seeing" changes in weather patterns over many years describes the changes in climate in the area where the tree grew.

4. Sample answer: I would use tree rings to analyze recent climate changes because trees are not typically as old as fossils. Trees might be as old as 100 or 200 years, but probably not older than that. Fossils are much older, more like thousands or even millions of years old and so would be better to use for analyzing climate change in the long ago past.

5. Sample answer: At the middle of the tree cross section would be rings that were fairly wide and spread apart. These would represent the oldest rings that grew early in the tree's life when rainfall was abundant. The rings would become narrower and narrower going farther toward the outside of the cross section. At the outermost region of the cross section the rings would be very narrow because the tree would not have been adding very many cells to its trunk in times of drought.

Unit Review
Vocabulary
1. **fossil** See Unit 2, Lesson 1
2. **half-life** See Unit 2, Lesson 3
3. **Continental drift** See Unit 2, Lesson 1
4. **Radioactive decay** See Unit 2, Lesson 3
5. **geology** See Unit 2, Lesson 4

Key Concepts
6. A   10. A
7. B   11. A
8. B   12. C
9. D   13. A

6. **A See Unit 2, Lesson 2**

A is correct because the top layer, layer 1, is the youngest.

B is incorrect because it is below layer 1, so it is older.

C is incorrect because it is below layer 2, so it is older.

D is incorrect because it is below layer 3, so it is the oldest.

7. **B See Unit 2, Lesson 3**

A is incorrect because the oldest glaciers are much younger than the Earth.

B is correct because this is how the age of the Earth is determined: by dating meteorites.

C is incorrect because the oldest fossils are younger than the Earth.

D is incorrect because determining the chemical

composition of sea-floor sediments will not tell you the age of the Earth.

8. B See Unit 2, Lesson 2

A is incorrect because a fossil at the top of the cliff is likely younger than one at the base.

B is correct because the fossil at the base of the cliff is likely older than any fossil found above it.

C is incorrect because a fossil halfway up the cliff is likely younger than one at the base.

D is incorrect because nothing in the question describes an index fossil.

9. D See Unit 2, Lesson 2

A is incorrect because the fault cuts through all of the layers and rocks, so it is the youngest feature.

B is incorrect because rock 1 cuts through rock 2, so rock 1 is younger.

C is incorrect because rock 2 cuts through layer 1, so rock 2 is younger.

D is correct because the fault, rock 1, and rock 2 cut through layer 1, so they formed after layer 1 formed.

10. A See Unit 2, Lesson 1

A is correct because both tracks and burrows form in soft sediment as a result of animal activities, and then may harden over time to form trace fossils.

B is incorrect because shells and bones are not trace fossils. They are the hard parts of an organism that are likely to become fossils.

C is incorrect because both the bee and beetle are not trace fossils. They are preserved specimens of whole organisms.

D is incorrect because petrified and mummified fossils do not result from the movement of an animal in soft sediment.

11. A See Unit 2, Lesson 1

A is correct because weathering and erosion break down, remove, and smooth bedrock in mountains over time.

B is incorrect because deposition is the process by which materials are deposited in some area over time.

C is incorrect because the movement of continents does not cause mountain ranges to become lower or more rounded over time.

D is incorrect because collisions between continental plates would most likely cause mountain ranges to form, rather than becoming lower and more rounded.

12. C See Unit 2, Lesson 1

A is incorrect because precipitation could not cause this arch to form.

B is incorrect because deposition is the process by which new materials are laid down, or deposited. This process does not form arches.

C is correct because wave action gradually eroded the rock to form an arch.

D is incorrect because volcanism is the process of transferring magma and hot, molten

material from Earth's interior to its surface as lava. This process does not form arches.

13. A See Unit 2, Lesson 3

A is correct because an index fossil is one of a known age range, so when found in a certain rock layer (or any rock unit) it can give a close estimate of the age.

B is incorrect because this is the description of a trace fossil.

C is incorrect because an amber fossil is not an index fossil.

D is incorrect because an animal caught in ice is not a fossil.

Critical Thinking

14. See Unit 2, Lesson 4

- Precambrian

- Paleozoic

- Mesozoic

- Cenozoic

- These divisions are based on major changes that occurred in Earth's history, such as the rise of mammals or mass extinctions that resulted from major environmental changes. These divisions help to organize the study of Earth's history.

15 See Unit 2, Lesson 3

- Radioactive decay is the process in which a radioactive isotope decays to a different isotope of that element or another element, emitting particles and energy.

- Half-life is the time required for half of a quantity of radioactive isotope to decay.

- Because radioactive decay occurs at a predictable rate, comparing the relative percentages of a radioactive (parent) isotope and a stable (daughter) isotope allows scientists to determine how long ago the rock formed.

Connect Essential Questions
16. See Unit 2, Lesson 1, Lesson 2, and Lesson 3

- Fossils can show what the environment was like at the time they existed. For example a fish fossil would indicate an aquatic environment. A tropical plant fossil would indicate a tropical past climate.

- Other materials, such as tree rings, can tell about past growing conditions. Sea-floor sediments and ice cores can tell us the past chemical compositions of the ocean and atmosphere. Ages of these can be found by radiometric dating techniques.

- For organic materials, radiocarbon dating could be used (45,000 years to present).

Unit Test A
Key Concepts
1. D   5. A   9. C
2. B   6. C   10. B
3. C   7. C   11. C
4. A   8. C   12. B

1. D

A   is incorrect because giving exact ages is using absolute dating, not relative dating.

B   is incorrect because it does not give their relative ages.

C   is incorrect because relative dating determines ages based on older or younger objects or events, not based on categories of objects.

D   is correct because Jacob's age is given with respect to the ages of his older brother and his younger sister, so their relative ages are known.

2. B

A   is incorrect because as uranium-238 decays, the amount of lead-206 would increase.

B   is correct because as uranium-238 decays, it would decrease. The lead-206 would increase.

C   is incorrect because as uranium-238 decays, it decreases.

D   is incorrect because lead-206 would increase as uranium-238 decreases.

3. C

A   is incorrect because nothing is stated about the geologists studying fossils.

B   is incorrect because a geologic record is Earth's geologic history, which the team was studying.

C   is correct because the team placed the rock layers in an ordered arrangement based on their relative ages.

D   is incorrect because a topographic map shows Earth's surface features.

4. A

A   is correct because the diagram shows a fossil of a fish.

B   is incorrect because an ice core is a long cylinder of ice obtained from a glacier or ice cap, and the image shows a fossil.

C   is incorrect because coprolites are fossilized dung, and the image shows the fossil of the body of a fish.

D   is incorrect because tree rings are structures in the cross-sections of tree trunks that indicate growth, and the image shows a fossil.

5. A

A   is correct because rock that contains fossils of organisms similar to those that live today is most likely younger than rock that contains fossils of species that lived long ago.

B   is incorrect because this property alone does not allow fossils to be used for relative dating.

C   is incorrect because this property does not allow scientists to determine the relative ages of the sedimentary layers.

D   is incorrect because it is rarely possible to determine a fossil's exact age; even if exact ages of fossils could be measured, this information is not needed to determine relative ages of rock layers.

6. C

A   is incorrect because geologic change is not rare. Instead, it tends to happen at a slow rate.

B   is incorrect because although sudden changes have affected Earth's surface, most geologic change tends to happen at a slow rate.

C is correct because uniformitarianism states that the same geologic processes have been re-sponsible for gradually shaping the Earth.

D is incorrect because although catastrophic events, such as asteroid collisions, have affected Earth's history, most geologic change tends to happen at a slow rate.

7. C

A is incorrect because the rock's age would reveal how old the rock is but not how it formed.

B is incorrect because although color might help identify an igneous rock (formed in a volcanic eruption), the color of a sedimentary rock does not generally provide clues about how the rock formed.

C is correct because the texture of a sedimentary rock can provide clues about how and where the rock formed.

D is incorrect because the fossils in a sedimentary rock would reveal the environment in which the rock formed but little about how the rock formed.

8. C

A is incorrect because the Eocene occurred before the most recent epoch, the Holocene.

B is incorrect because the Pliocene occurred before the most recent epoch, the Holocene.

C is correct because the Holocene is the most recent epoch.

D is incorrect because the Pleistocene preceded the Holocene.

9. C

A is incorrect because the formation of Earth marks the beginning of Precambrian time.

B is incorrect because the extinction of the dinosaurs marks the end of the Cretaceous Period.

C is correct because the first animals with exoskeletons appear in the fossil record just after the end of Precambrian time.

D is incorrect because the largest mass extinction in Earth's history marks the end of the Permian Period.

10. B

A is incorrect because a bone is a structure that may be fossilized as a result of having been preserved in rock, ice, amber, or hardened asphalt.

B is correct because a trace fossil is a structure, such as tracks or dung, that form as a result of an organism's activity on soft sediment.

C is incorrect because a frozen fossil is a structure, such as skin, bones, and fur that are found in ice.

D is incorrect because a petrified fossil is a structure, such as bone, that forms as

the result of minerals replacing soft body tissues.

11. C

A is incorrect because early proponents of catastrophism thought that significant changes on Earth's surface must be caused by sudden catastrophic events.

B is incorrect because at the time not enough was known about Earth's structure for its evolution to become part of the debate.

C is correct because early proponents of catastrophism thought that significant changes on Earth's surface must be caused by catastrophic events.

D is incorrect because this describes the idea of uniformitarianism.

12. B

A is incorrect because half-life is the number of years it takes for half of the parent isotope in a sample to break down into daughter isotope.

B is correct because any method used for absolute dating measures the age in years of an object.

C is incorrect because radiocarbon dating can only be used to date organic material.

D is incorrect because the age of an index fossil cannot be directly determined by an absolute dating method. Instead, it can be dated from the ages of the strata above and below it.

Critical Thinking
13.

- moon rocks or meteorites
- moon rocks and some meteorites are older than the oldest rocks on Earth

Extended Response
14.

- intrusion younger than Layer B
- law of crosscutting relationships
- from oldest to youngest: Q, B, N
- law of superposition

Unit Test B
Key Concepts

1. A	5. B	9. D
2. D	6. A	10. B
3. B	7. C	11. B
4. D	8. D	12. A

1. A

A is correct because relative dating is a comparison of different ages.

B is incorrect because differences in height cannot always be correlated to differences in age.

C is incorrect because differences in weight cannot always be correlated to differences in age.

D is incorrect because the month of birth cannot be used to compare ages for siblings that were born in different years.

2. D

A is incorrect because the relative amounts of the two isotopes are needed rather than just the mass of the uranium-238 isotope.

B is incorrect because the relative amounts of the two isotopes are needed rather than just the amount of the lead-206 isotope.

C is incorrect because radiometric dating uses the relative amounts of the isotopes, not the en-ergy released from the radioactive isotope.

D is correct because radiometric dating uses the relative percentages of the parent and daughter isotope to determine the age of the sample.

3. B

A is incorrect because a geologic column is not constructed based on surface features.

B is correct because a geologic column is constructed by comparing the types of rock and the kinds of fossils that are in each rock layer.

C is incorrect because a geologic column can be made using relative dating methods.

D is incorrect because rock layers from different areas are compared to make a geologic column.

4. D

A is incorrect because the fish species could still exist.

B is incorrect because there is not enough information provided about the relative age of the fossil.

C is incorrect because fossils are usually found in sedimentary rock.

D is correct because the fish fossil indicates that the rocks were once under water.

5. B

A is incorrect because comparing the fossils in a single layer does not help scientists learn when other layers were deposited, which is needed in order to determine the relative ages of the layers.

B is correct because by comparing known fossils in many different rock layers, scientists can infer the relative ages of the layers based on knowledge of when the various fossilized species lived on Earth.

C is incorrect because the position of fossils do not help scientists learn relative ages of rock layers; only by comparing different fossils in different rock layers can scientists learn about relative ages of the layers.

D is incorrect because although scientists can learn about the relative age of rock layers by comparing fossils in rock layers around the world, simply locating those areas is not helpful.

6. A

A is correct because erosion changes the land surface continuously over geologic time.

B is incorrect because extinction events are short-lived and do not happen continuously.

C is incorrect because earthquakes are short-lived and do not happen continuously.

D is incorrect because volcanic eruptions are short-lived and do not happen continuously.

7. C

A is incorrect because quartz is a mineral that is found in sedimentary rock, but is not a type of sedimentary rock.

B is incorrect because calcite is a mineral that is found in sedimentary rock, but is not a type of sedimentary rock.

C is correct because limestone forms from the remains of animals that lived in the ocean.

D is incorrect because sandstone forms when sand grains become cemented together.

8. D

A is incorrect because the Tertiary Period preceded the most recent period, the Quaternary Period.

B is incorrect because the Holocene is the most recent epoch, not the most recent period.

C is incorrect because the Cenozoic is the most recent era, not the most recent period.

D is correct because the most recent period is the Quaternary Period.

9. D

A is incorrect because the extinction of the dinosaurs marks the end of the Cretaceous Period.

B is incorrect because the first bipedal human ancestor appears at the beginning of the Pleistocene Epoch.

C is incorrect because the first animals with exoskeletons appear in the fossil record just after the end of Precambrian time.

D is correct because the largest mass extinction in Earth's history marks the end of the Permian Period.

10. B

A is incorrect because shells and bones are the hard parts of an organism that are likely to become fossils.

B is correct because both tracks and burrows form in soft sediment as a result of animal activities, and then may harden over time to form trace fossils.

C is incorrect because both the bee and the beetle are preserved specimens of whole organisms.

D is incorrect because petrified and mummified fossils do not result from the movement of an animal in soft sediment.

11. B

A is incorrect because scientists now recognize that Earth's surface is reshaped by both sudden and gradual geologic processes.

B is correct because scientists now recognize that Earth's surface is reshaped by both sudden and gradual geologic processes.

C is incorrect because scientists now recognize that Earth's surface is reshaped by both sudden and gradual geologic processes.

D is incorrect because both slow and rapid geologic processes have occurred throughout Earth's history.

12. A

A is correct because absolute dating includes different methods that scientists use to measure the age of rock.

B is incorrect because scientists study physical structure using methods such as microscopic analysis, not absolute dating.

C is incorrect because scientists study composition using methods of chemical analysis, not absolute dating.

D is incorrect because scientists study geographic distribution using field surveys and other methods, not absolute dating.

Critical Thinking
13.

• meteorites (and some lunar rocks) have been dated as older than Earth's oldest rocks (e.g., *Meteor-ites that have hit Earth have been dated using radiometric methods*; etc.)

• Earth formed at an earlier time than the age of its oldest rocks, because the rocks that first formed on Earth have been exposed to erosion and other geologic processes over billions of years (e.g., *They are useful for determining the age of Earth because the first rocks that formed on Earth have long ago been eroded or melted, or buried under younger rocks. Other bodies in space such as meteorites do contain rocks that are as old our solar system*; etc.).

Extended Response

14.

- intrusion younger than Layer Q

- the law of crosscutting relationships (e.g., *The law of crosscutting relationships states that a rock body is younger than any other body of rock that it cuts through. Therefore, the intrusion is younger than the layer 1, since the intrusion cuts through layer 1*; etc.)

- from oldest to youngest: Q, B, N, Intrusion

- the law of crosscutting relationships, the law of superposition (e.g., *Layer Q formed first, then Layer B, and then Layer N according to the law of superposition. The intrusion formed after the three layers according to the law of crosscutting relationships;* etc.)

Unit 3 Minerals and Rocks

Unit Pretest

1. C	5. C	9. D
2. D	6. A	10. D
3. B	7. A	
4. A	8. A	

1. C

A is incorrect because the term foliated applies to banded metamorphic rocks.

B is incorrect because the term intrusive applies to igneous rocks that form below Earth's surface.

C is correct because the term extrusive describes igneous rocks that form on Earth's as a result of a volcanic eruption.

D is incorrect because the term nonfoliated applies to metamorphic rocks that lack a banded texture.

2. D

A is incorrect because erosion describes weathered material that is being transported from one place to another.

B is incorrect because deposition describes eroded material that is being laid down.

C is incorrect because subsidence describes the sinking of Earth's crust to a lower elevation.

D is correct because weathering causes rocks to break into fragments.

3. B

A is incorrect because this could describe either foliated or nonfoliated texture.

B is correct because foliation is the arrangement of mineral grains into bands or planes.

C is incorrect because this describes nonfoliated texture.

D is incorrect because this could describe either foliated or nonfoliated texture.

4. A

A is correct because the unknown mineral scratched apatite, which means that it is as hard or harder than apatite. Two minerals that scratch each other have the same hardness.

B is incorrect because the unknown mineral scratched apatite, which means that the mineral cannot be calcite. Calcite is softer than apatite.

C is incorrect because the unknown mineral scratched apatite, which means that the mineral cannot be fluorite. Fluorite is softer than apatite.

D is incorrect because the unknown mineral scratched both calcite and apatite, which means that the mineral cannot be gypsum. Gypsum is softer than both calcite and apatite.

5. C

A is incorrect because it is common for igneous rocks to become metamorphic rocks over time.

B is incorrect because it is common for rocks to melt and become molten rock again.

C is correct because rocks constantly change over long periods of time, so it is most unlikely that most of the basalt would have stayed the same for 2 billion years.

D is incorrect because it is common for rocks to weather and become sediment.

6. A

A is correct because the rising of Earth's crust to a higher elevation is known as uplift, which can happen when tectonic plates collide.

B is incorrect because erosion is the process that transports soil and sediments to a different location.

C is incorrect because deposition takes place when new materials are laid down.

D is incorrect because the rising of Earth's crust to a higher elevation is known as uplift, and subsidence is the sinking of Earth's crust to a lower elevation.

7. A

A is correct because the three major types of sedimentary rock are chemical, clastic, and organic.

B is incorrect because inorganic is not a type of sedimentary rock.

C is incorrect because nonfoliated is not a type of sedimentary rock.

D is incorrect because crystalline not a type of sedimentary rock.

8. A

A is correct because matter is anything that has mass and takes up space, and the container is holding extra mass.

B is incorrect because he cannot tell what state of matter the

container holds simply by finding its mass.

C is incorrect because energy does not have mass, and the container is holding 0.7 g of mass.

D is incorrect because he cannot tell what state of matter the container holds based only its mass.

9. D

A is incorrect because native elements are composed of only one element and are not compounds.

B is incorrect because native elements are composed of only one element and are not compounds.

C is incorrect because native elements are composed of only one element and are not compounds.

D is correct because native elements are made up of only one element.

10. D

A is incorrect because if the rocks formed from cooling magma, the rocks would be igneous and not sedimentary.

B is incorrect because heat and pressure do not create layers of material but fuse all of the materials together to form metamorphic rock.

C is incorrect because if the rocks formed from cooling lava, the rocks would be igneous and not sedimentary.

D is correct because sedimentary rock forms as layers of sediment harden over time.

Lesson 1 Quiz

1. B 4. D
2. B 5. C
3. C

1. B

A is incorrect because some kinds of matter, such as a neutral atom, have no charge.

B is correct because matter is anything that has mass and takes up space.

C is incorrect because some particles of matter, such as a proton or neutron, are only parts of what might make up an atom.

D is incorrect because some kinds of matter, such as ionic compounds like sodium chloride (ta-ble salt), do not consist of molecules, nor is temperature a defining characteristic of matter.

2. B

A is incorrect because gold is a native element.

B is correct because mica is made up of mostly silicon and oxygen atoms.

C is incorrect because halite is a salt crystal made up of sodium and chloride.

D is incorrect because oxygen is not a mineral.

3. C

A is incorrect because all other minerals are softer than diamond.

B is incorrect because many minerals, such as calcite and gypsum, are common and inexpensive.

C is correct because all minerals have an orderly internal crystal structure.

D is incorrect because many minerals, such as quartz, do not contain carbon atoms.

4. D

A is incorrect because it describes how minerals in igneous rocks form.

B is incorrect because it describes how minerals in hydrothermal metamorphic rocks form.

C is incorrect because it describes how minerals in contact with metamorphic rocks form.

D is correct because caves formed from the dissolving and depositing of limestone minerals by water can produce stalagmites and stalactites.

5. C

A is incorrect because calcite has cleavage along three different planes, but they are not at right angles and thus do not produce a cube.

B is incorrect because fluorite forms a octahedron, not a cube.

C is correct because halite has cleavage along three different planes that are at right angles and thus could produce a cube.

D is incorrect because muscovite has cleavage along only one plane, so it produces only flat, asymmetrical shapes.

Lesson 2 Quiz

1. B   4. B
2. C   5. C
3. C

1. B

A is incorrect because erosion is the transport of soil and sediments to new locations.

B is correct because the ash falling to Earth's surface is an example of deposition.

C is incorrect because subsidence is the sinking of regions of the Earth's crust.

D is incorrect because weathering is the disintegration and decomposition of rocks.

2. C

A is incorrect because cooling takes place when magma forms igneous rock.

B is incorrect because melting changes rock into magma.

C is correct because sediment is deposited and then hardens under pressure to form sedimentary rock.

D is incorrect because weathering can change metamorphic rock into sediment, but it cannot change sediment into sedimentary rock.

3. B

A is incorrect because the addition of groundwater would serve to further weigh down the crust.

B is correct because the crust subsides when massive amounts of rock material or ice are depos-ited in one location.

C is incorrect because the momentum of the sediment as it is transported is very slight compared to the mass of the crust.

D is incorrect because the crust must react to the additional weight of the sediment by subsiding.

4. B

A is incorrect because Earth's crust rising to a higher elevation is the definition for *uplift* rather than *subsidence*.

B is correct because *subsidence* is defined as Earth's crust sinking to a lower elevation.

C is incorrect because *subsidence* is defined as Earth's crust sinking rather than shifting sideways.

D is incorrect because *subsidence* specifically refers to the movement of Earth's crust to a lower elevation.

5. C

A is incorrect because the color is not an indication of how the rock was formed.

B is incorrect because all rocks are relatively hard.

C is correct because the layers suggest that the rock formed as sediments in their distinct layers hardened to form rock.

D is incorrect because the location where the rock was found cannot be used as a means of identifying the rock type.

Lesson 3 Quiz

1. A   3. B   5. D
2. D   4. A

1. A

A   is correct because clastic sedimentary rocks are made of fragments of other rocks that have been broken down and transported.

B   is incorrect because organic sedimentary rocks form from the remains of organisms, not sediments.

C   is incorrect because foliated rocks are metamorphic rocks that have a banded texture due to high pressure.

D   is incorrect because extrusive rocks are igneous rocks the form as a result of volcanic eruptions.

2. D

A   is incorrect because clasts are fragments of rock that form sedimentary rock.

B   is incorrect because magma forms igneous rock.

C   is incorrect because sediments form sedimentary rock.

D   is correct because metamorphism can change any type of existing rock into metamorphic rock.

3. B

A   is incorrect because granite is igneous rock, and gneiss is metamorphic rock.

B   is correct because granite forms from cooling magma, so it is igneous. Gneiss forms after heat and pressure

change the rock, which makes it metamorphic.

C   is incorrect because the change is from igneous rock to metamorphic rock.

D   is incorrect because granite forms when magma cools, so granite is igneous rock rather than sedimentary rock.

4. A

A   is correct because crystals grow larger with time.

B   is incorrect because crystals grow larger with time.

C   is incorrect because the cooling of magma does not cause foliated texture.

D   is incorrect because the cooling of magma does not cause foliated texture.

5. D

A   is incorrect because minerals are not inorganic.

B   is incorrect because minerals are not synthetic.

C   is incorrect because minerals are always crystals.

D   is correct because rocks can be either crystalline or noncrystalline, but minerals are always crystals by definition.

Lesson 1 Alternative Assessment

You Ask the Questions: Quizzes contain at least six questions (of different types) about the ways minerals can form.

Trading Definitions: Cards identify, picture, and define elements, atoms, and compounds, and include a few examples.

Distinguished Work: Collages distinguishes between minerals and nonminerals, and describes the characteristics of each.

Presenting Properties: Presentations compare and contrast properties of common minerals, and include illustrations or diagrams.

You Decide: Cards tell what student know about minerals before reviewing the lesson, and what student learned about minerals.

Picturing Minerals: Posters show common minerals and describe the characteristics of minerals.

Pair Match Up: Cards describe physical properties of minerals. Matching cards include information that pairs only with one mineral.

What Am I?: Skits portray two different minerals and their properties.

Guess the Mineral: Game show ways to identify minerals. Cards name minerals and describe how to identify them.

Lesson 2 Alternative Assessment

Igneous rock: Igneous rock and the way it is formed are correctly identified.

Sedimentary rock: Sedimentary rock and the way it is formed are correctly identified.

Metamorphic rock: Metamorphic rock and the way it is formed are correctly identified.

Weathering: Weathering and at least two of its possible causes are identified.

Erosion: Erosion is correctly identified and its causes are discussed.

Deposition: Deposition is correctly identified and its causes are discussed.

Lesson 3 Alternative Assessment

Rock and Roll: How rock is classified should be clearly described; additionally, the three classes of rock should be accurately described. Presentation of song can be recorded or live.

Rockin' Art: How each of the three classes of rock—igneous, sedimentary, and metamorphic—forms should be clearly described. Posters should include labels or captions that give details and examples.

Pet Rock: Type of rock should be accurately identified, and details of where it was found and how its identification was made should be included.

Rock Models: Models should possess accurate features and details for each type of rock. Presentation should include labels with information about how each rock type formed, and where each type could be realistically be found.

Take a Hike: Samples should be accurately identified. Presentation should include labels to identify the type of rock and give details of how this identification was made.

Floating Rock: The process that forms pumice should be clearly described, and an accurate explanation of why it floats should be given.

Rock Puzzle: At least 15 terms should be included in the puzzle, and clues should give clear, accurate information about each term used in the puzzle.

Movie Rocks: The process that forms each type of rock should be clearly shown, along with accurate information on how subtypes of each type of rock are formed.

Performance-Based Assessment

See Unit 3, Lesson 1

1-4. Check students' data tables for accuracy. Answers will vary depending on samples selected to test.

5. Check to make sure students' correctly identified the samples you provided.

6. Answers will vary. Sample answer: I did not test density, cleavage, or fluorescence. I could find the mass and volume of the mineral and use that to find the density, I can check to see fracture and cleavage, and I can use a UV light to determine fluorescence.

7. Answers will vary. Sample answer: No. I may have been able to make a guess, but testing more characteristics ensured that I was identifying the mineral correctly.

Unit Review
Vocabulary
1. **Rock cycle** See Unit 3, Lesson 2
2. **Metamorphic** See Unit 3, Lesson 2
3. **rock** See Unit 3, Lesson 3
4. **uplift** See Unit 3, Lesson 2
5. **Luster** See Unit 3, Lesson 1

Key Concepts
6. D	9. B	12. B
7. A	10. B	
8. D	11. B	

6. D See Unit 3, Lesson 1

A   is incorrect because feldspars are silicate minerals, which contain silicate tetrahedrons.

B   is incorrect because micas are silicate minerals, which contain silicate tetrahedrons.

C   is incorrect because the table lists only nonsilicate minerals.

D   is correct because sulfates contain compounds of sulfur and oxygen and so are nonsilicate minerals.

7. A See Unit 3, Lesson 3

A   is correct because granite and basalt are both igneous rock; both form when molten rock cools and forms a solid.

B   is incorrect because they are not minerals

C   is incorrect because they are not fossils.

D   is incorrect because basalt is not intrusive.

8. D See Unit 3, Lesson 1

A   is incorrect because cleavage is the tendency of a mineral to break along specific planes of weakness to form smooth, flat surfaces.

B is incorrect because color is determined visually and not by scratching it against a plate to determine streak.

C is incorrect because luster describes how the surface of a mineral reflects light.

D is correct because streak is the color of a mineral in a powdered form. Streak is observed by rubbing the mineral across a porcelain plate, called a streak plate.

9. B See Unit 3, Lesson 1

A is incorrect because elements are made of atoms which can form compounds.

B is correct because compounds are not smaller than atoms.

C is incorrect because elements and compounds do form the basis for all materials.

D is incorrect because an atom is a substance that cannot be broken down into smaller substances.

10. B See Unit 3, Lesson 3

A is incorrect because this process describes how intrusive igneous rock forms.

B is correct because most sedimentary rock is formed when materials are deposited in layers and compacted over time due to accumulating pressure.

C is incorrect because this process describes how metamorphic rock is formed.

D is incorrect because this process describes how extrusive igneous rock forms.

11. B See Unit 3, Lesson 2

A is incorrect because the two plates are moving in opposite directions, away from each other.

B is correct because a rift zone is an area where two plates move away from each other and form a rift zone as in the picture.

C is incorrect because the two plates are moving in opposite directions, away from each other.

D is incorrect because the area when two plates are moving away from each other, mountain building does not occur between them.

12. B See Unit 3, Lesson 2

A is incorrect because subsidence describes the sinking of Earth's crust to a lower elevation.

B is correct because weathering, such as freeze-thaw, causes rocks to break down.

C is incorrect because deposition describes eroded material that is being laid down.

D is incorrect because erosion describes weathered material that is being transported from one place to another.

Critical Thinking
13. See Unit 3, Lesson 1

- The area was either once an inland sea or covered by ocean water. During the ocean's retreat or the inland sea's evaporation, sediments and shells were deposited to the ground. They compacted and

became cemented over time, and eventually became a sedimentary rock layer.

14. See Unit 3, Lesson 2

- Sedimentary and igneous rock must undergo chemical changes due to heat (for example, contact metamorphism) or heat and pressure (for example, burial) to turn into metamorphic rock.

- This could occur by contact metamorphism, where a magma body heats the rock around it and changes this rock. It could occur by repeated deposition on top of a rock unit, burying it over time. This layer experiences heat and pressure of varying degrees throughout this process, slowly changing into a metamorphic rock.

Connect Essential Questions
15. See Unit 3, Lesson 2 and Lesson 3

- Sedimentary rocks form when rock is broken down into smaller pieces by the process of weathering.

- This sedimentary rock is weathered and eroded by wind, precipitation, and temperature changes over a very long period of time.

- The sediment can be eroded and transported to another location by a river or glacier (accept any reasonable), where it is eventually deposited in layers.

- This deposit is compacted over time due to accumulating

pressure of sediments deposited on top of it. The layers of sediment can become sedimentary rocks again if subjected to compression.

Unit Test A
Key Concepts
1. D   5. D   9. A
2. B   6. D   10. B
3. B   7. B   11. C
4. C   8. B   12. B

1. D

A is incorrect because acid rain causes weathering, not erosion.

B is incorrect because acid rain causes weathering, not erosion.

C is incorrect because acid rain causes more weathering than normal rainwater does.

D is correct because acid rain is better able to dissolve the minerals in rocks, which speeds up the weathering process.

2. B

A is incorrect because weathering does not change a sedimentary rock into a metamorphic rock.

B is correct because the sedimentary rock, shale, changes into the metamorphic rock, slate, after exposure to heat and pressure.

C is incorrect because erosion and deposition do not change a sedimentary rock into a metamorphic rock.

D is incorrect because melting and solidification do not change a sedimentary rock into a metamorphic rock.

3. B

A is incorrect because subduction happens where one tectonic plate slides under another.

B is correct because magma flows upward at the center of a rift zone as the two plates move apart.

C is incorrect because the diagram shows magma moving upward, not lava solidifying.

D is incorrect because the rift zone forms as two oceanic plates diverge.

4. C

A is incorrect because texture is not determined by the colors of the grains that make up a rock.

B is incorrect because texture is not determined by the densities of the grains that make up a rock.

C is correct because the texture of a rock is described by its appearance in terms of the sizes, shapes, and positions of the grains that make up the rock.

D is incorrect because texture is not determined by the compositions of the grains that make up a rock.

5. D

A is incorrect because only igneous minerals form from as a result of melting.

B is incorrect because only igneous minerals form from as a result of melting.

C is incorrect because only igneous minerals form from as a result of melting.

D is correct because metamorphic minerals form when existing minerals are changed by variations in temperature, pressure, chemical makeup, or any combination of these factors.

6. D

A is incorrect because when an igneous rock forms, magma cools and changes from a liquid to a solid.

B is incorrect because when an igneous rock forms, magma cools and changes from a liquid to a solid.

C is incorrect because when an igneous rock forms, magma cools and changes from a liquid to a solid.

D is correct because when an igneous rock forms, magma cools and changes from liquid to solid rock.

7. B

A is incorrect because the feldspar sample has a mass of 16 g divided by a volume of 6.2 mL to equal a density of 2.6 g/mL.

B is correct because the galena sample has a mass of 9 g divided by a volume of 1.2 mL to equal a density of 7.5 g/mL.

C is incorrect because the garnet sample has a mass of 12 g divided by a volume of 3.0 mL to equal a density of 4.0 g/mL.

D is incorrect because the quartz sample has a mass of 10 g divided by a volume of 3.7 mL to equal a density of 2.7 g/mL.

8. B

A is incorrect because nonminerals can contain silicon and oxygen.

B is correct because minerals are crystalline, which means they have an orderly internal structure.

C is incorrect because minerals often contain more than one type of atom.

D is incorrect because the number of atoms in a ring does not determine whether something is a mineral.

9. A

A is correct because basalt forms from the cooling of lava on Earth's surface, and because granite forms from the cooling of magma below the surface.

B is incorrect because basalt forms from the cooling of lava on Earth's surface, and because granite forms from the cooling of magma below the surface.

C is incorrect because granite forms from the cooling of magma below the surface, not as a result of cementation.

D is incorrect because basalt forms from the cooling of lava on Earth's surface, not as a result of cementation.

10. B

A is incorrect because neither conglomerate, sandstone, nor

siltstone forms as a result of evaporation.

B is correct because conglomerate, sandstone, and siltstone are all made of clasts that have been cemented together.

C is incorrect because neither conglomerate, sandstone, nor siltstone forms as a result of the cooling and solidification of molten rock.

D is incorrect because neither conglomerate, sandstone, nor siltstone forms as a result of the condensation of solid material out of a gas.

11. C

A is incorrect because the diagram shows rock layers being deformed, not the intrusion of magma.

B is incorrect because the diagram shows rock layers being deformed, not the eruption of magma.

C is correct because the diagram show rock layers being deformed under high pressure.

D is incorrect because chemical sedimentary rocks do not form deep below Earth's surface.

12. B

A is incorrect because erosion leads to deposition, which forms sedimentary rock, not igneous rock.

B is correct because only igneous rocks forms from the cooling of liquid rock.

C is incorrect because deposition can form both igneous and sedimentary rocks.

D is incorrect because metamorphism can only form metamorphic rock.

Critical Thinking

13.

- inorganic substance
- characteristic chemical composition

Extended Response

14.

- both made of atoms
- compounds include two or more elements
- example of native element (e.g., *gold*; etc.)
- example of native mineral that is a compound (e.g., *quartz*; etc.)

Unit Test B

Key Concepts

1. C	5. B	9. C
2. C	6. A	10. A
3. C	7. C	11. D
4. B	8. B	12. A

1. C

A is incorrect because the rate at which acid rain dissolves rock depends on the chemical composition of the rock.

B is incorrect because dissolving sedimentary or igneous rocks does not cause metamorphic rocks to form.

C is correct because the rate at which acid rain dissolves rock depends on the chemical composition of the rock.

D is incorrect because dissolving is not the same as melting.

2. C

A is incorrect because adding heat does not change a metamorphic rock into a sedimentary rock.

B is incorrect because adding pressure does not change a metamorphic rock into a sedimentary rock.

C is correct because erosion and deposition can change a metamorphic rock into a sedimentary rock.

D is incorrect because melting and solidification do not change a metamorphic rock into a sedimentary rock.

3. C

A is incorrect because a rift zone is an area where two plates are moving away from each other at a divergent boundary.

B is incorrect because a rift zone forms at a divergent boundary.

C is correct because a rift zone forms in an area where two plates are pulling away from each other.

D is incorrect because a rift zone is an area where two plates are moving away from each other, not where a plate is falling or rising relative to the other.

4. B

A is incorrect because the term organic refers to the composition of a rock, not its texture.

B is correct because the term foliated is used to describe the banded texture of metamorphic rocks.

C is incorrect because the term intrusive refers to the way a rock forms, not its texture.

D is incorrect because the term light-colored refers to the composition of a rock, not its texture.

5. B

A is incorrect because both types of minerals can change their composition as they form.

B is correct because magma is liquid rock, and metamorphic minerals form from changes to existing minerals without melting them.

C is incorrect because both igneous and metamorphic minerals can be altered by intense pressure.

D is incorrect because the manner in which minerals form does not determine their temperature.

6. A

A is correct because weathering breaks down igneous rock so that it can eventually become sedimentary rock.

B is incorrect because when an igneous rock deforms, it becomes a metamorphic rock.

C is incorrect because when pressure increases on an igneous rock, it can deform and become metamorphic rock.

D is incorrect because lowering the temperature of an igneous rock will not cause it to change into a sedimentary rock; it must first be physically or chemically broken down.

7. C

A is incorrect because the unknown sample has a density of 4.0 g/mL, and feldspar has a density of 2.6 g/mL.

B is incorrect because the unknown sample has a density of 4.0 g/mL, and galena has a density of 7.5 g/mL.

C is correct because the unknown sample has a density of 4.0 g/mL, and garnet has a density of 4.0 g/mL.

D is incorrect because the unknown sample has a density of 4.0 g/mL, and quartz has a density of 2.7 g/mL.

8. B

A is incorrect because a silicate mineral must contain both oxygen and silicon atoms and cannot be a combination of only oxygen and any other element.

B is correct because a mineral has an orderly arrangement of atoms, which in silicate minerals include atoms of silicon and oxygen.

C is incorrect because it is too general; silicate minerals specifically include silicon and oxygen atoms.

D is incorrect because a mineral must have an orderly arrangement of atoms.

9. C

A is incorrect because basalt is an igneous rock, and therefore cannot be organic, and because granite is an igneous rock, and therefore cannot be clastic.

B is incorrect because basalt is an igneous rock, and therefore cannot be clastic, and because granite is an igneous rock, and therefore cannot be organic.

C is correct because basalt forms from the cooling of lava that is extruded onto Earth's surface, and because granite forms form the cooling of magma that is intruded below Earth's surface.

D is incorrect because basalt forms from the cooling of lava that is extruded onto Earth's surface, and because granite forms form the cooling of magma that is intruded below Earth's surface.

10. A

A is correct because conglomerate, sandstone, and siltstone are all made of clasts.

B is incorrect because conglomerate, sandstone, and siltstone are all made of clasts, not the remains or organisms.

C is incorrect because the term foliated only applies to metamorphic rocks with a banded texture.

D is incorrect because conglomerate, sandstone, and

siltstone form from the cementation of clasts, not the precipitation of minerals out of a solution.

11. D

A is incorrect because erosion only occurs on Earth's surface.

B is incorrect because the diagram does not show magma.

C is incorrect because weathering only occurs on Earth's surface.

D is correct because the diagram shows rock layers being deformed by high pressure conditions.

12. A

A is correct because erosion leads to deposition, which forms sedimentary rock.

B is incorrect because only igneous rocks form from the cooling of liquid rock.

C is incorrect because subduction causes metamorphism and melting.

D is incorrect because metamorphism can only form metamorphic rock.

Critical Thinking

13.

- naturally occurring

- solid with orderly internal structure (crystals)

Extended Response

14.

- compounds, not elements, can be broken down by into simpler substances by chemical means, or compounds include

two or more elements

- quartz as compound

- gold as element

- diamond as element

Unit 4 The Restless Earth

Unit Pretest

1. C	5. B	9. B
2. A	6. A	10. C
3. B	7. B	
4. D	8. C	

1. C

A is incorrect because the epicenter and focus are switched.

B is incorrect because the epicenter and focus are switched, and because the seismic wave and fault are switched.

C is correct because it correctly assigns the labels on the diagram.

D is incorrect because the seismic wave and fault are switched.

2. A

A is correct because the core is the central part of Earth.

B is incorrect because the crust is the outermost layer of Earth.

C is incorrect because the lithosphere is the solid outer physical layer of Earth that is made up of the crust and the upper part of the mantle.

D is incorrect because the mesosphere is the slow-flowing lower part of the mantle; it is not in the center of Earth.

3. B

A   is incorrect because a shield volcano is formed by quiet eruptions.

B   is correct because composite volcanoes are formed by alternating quiet and violent eruptions.

C   is incorrect because pyroclastic is a type of volcanic material rather than a type of volcano.

D   is incorrect because a cinder cone volcano is formed by violent eruptions.

4. D

A   is incorrect because a caldera, or deep depression, forms following a volcanic eruption.

B   is incorrect because volcanoes often occur at plate boundaries, but they do not form plate boundaries.

C   is incorrect because a magma chamber forms beneath Earth's surface.

D   is correct because a volcanic mountain forms when lava builds up, on Earth's surface, over time.

5. B

A   is incorrect because a syncline is a kind of fold in which the youngest rock layers are in the center of the fold.

B   is correct because an anticline is a kind of fold in which the oldest rock layers are in the center of the fold.

C   is incorrect because both synclines and anticlines can be symmetrical folds.

D   is incorrect because both synclines and anticlines can be asymmetrical folds.

6. A

A   is correct because oceanic crust contains much more iron, calcium, and magnesium than continental crust and is therefore more dense than continental crust.

B   is incorrect because the shading indicates that continental crust is less dense than oceanic crust.

C   is incorrect because the shading indicates that oceanic crust is more dense than continental crust, which is in part because oceanic crust contains more iron than continental crust.

D   is incorrect because the shading indicates that oceanic crust is more dense than continental crust, which is in part because oceanic crust contains more magnesium than continental crust.

7. B

A   is incorrect because conduction is the transfer of energy as heat between two objects that are in contact with each other.

B   is correct because convection current is established as molten rock rises, cools, and then sinks.

C   is incorrect because conduction is the transfer of energy as heat within an object.

D   is incorrect because energy as heat always flows from a

warmer area or object to a cooler area or object.

8. C

A   is incorrect because tension stretches rocks apart and makes them break, not fold.

B   is incorrect because, although some shear stress is involved as mountains fold, the primary cause of the folding is compression.

C   is correct because folded mountains form when compression at convergent tectonic plate boundaries folds and uplifts rock layers.

D   is incorrect because volcanic activity, although it can build mountains, does not build folded mountains.

9. B

A   is incorrect because Earth is divided into these five layers based on physical properties, not core properties.

B   is correct because Earth is divided into these five layers based on physical properties.

C   is incorrect because Earth is divided into these five layers based on physical properties, not chemical properties.

D   is incorrect because Earth is divided into these five layers based on physical properties, not atmospheric properties.

10. C

A   is incorrect because plates pull apart at divergent boundaries.

B   is incorrect because plates pull apart at divergent boundaries, which would increase rock deformation.

C is correct because convergence takes place when plates move toward one another.

D is incorrect because plates slide horizontally past each other along Earth's surface at a transform boundary.

Lesson 1 Quiz

1. C   3. D   5. D
2. A   4. B

1. C

A is incorrect because the outer core is a liquid surrounding the solid, inner core.

B is incorrect because the lithosphere is the solid, outer layer of Earth that consists of the crust and the rigid, upper part of the mantle.

C is correct because the mesosphere is the lower part of the mantle where materials flow slowly.

D is incorrect because the asthenosphere is the soft layer of the mantle on which the tectonic plates move.

2. A

A is correct because the crust is the thinnest layer of Earth.

B is incorrect because the crust is much thinner than the mantle is.

C is incorrect because the crust is much thinner than the inner core is, and the inner core is a physical layer.

D is incorrect because the crust is much thinner than the outer core is, and the outer core is a physical layer.

3. D

A is incorrect because there are five physical layers and only three compositional layers.

B is incorrect because all of the compositional layers are included in the physical layers.

C is incorrect because the lithosphere, not the asthenosphere, includes the compositional layer of the crust.

D is correct because the physical layers of the inner core and outer core are both included in the compositional layer of the core.

4. B

A is incorrect because the outer core is liquid, and the inner core is solid.

B is correct because the outer core is liquid, and the inner core is solid.

C is incorrect because the inner and outer cores are made of both nickel and iron.

D is incorrect because the inner and outer cores are made of both nickel and iron.

5. D

A is incorrect because the core, the mantle, and the crust are based on chemical composition, not their relative density.

B is incorrect because the core, the mantle, and the crust are based on chemical composition, not their physical structure.

C is incorrect because the core, the mantle, and the crust are based on chemical composition, not geographical location.

D is correct because the core, the mantle, and the crust are based on their chemical composition.

Lesson 2 Quiz

1. D   3. B   5. B
2. C   4. A

1. D

A is incorrect because sea-floor spreading describes the movement of tectonic plates away from mid-ocean ridges, but does not describe the mechanism of the movement.

B is incorrect because a convection current transfers heat and continental drift is the hypothesis that Earth's continents once formed a single landmass, but it does not explain how tectonic plates move.

C is incorrect because sea-floor spreading describes the movement of tectonic plates away from mid-ocean ridges, and continental drift is the hypothesis that Earth's continents once formed a single landmass, but neither explains how tectonic plates move.

D is correct because mantle convection, ridge push, and slab pull are the three mechanisms that have been proposed to explain the movement of tectonic plates.

2. C

A is incorrect because tectonic plate motion would be felt if it occurred at a rate of meters/day.

B   is incorrect because tectonic plate motion would be felt if it occurred at a rate of meters/week.

C   is correct because this rate of motion cannot be seen or felt without the use of specialized instruments, such as satellites.

D   is incorrect because tectonic plate motion would be felt if it occurred at a rate of kilometers/month.

3.   B

A   is incorrect because oceanic crust is thinner than continental crust.

B   is correct because continental crust is thicker than oceanic crust.

C   is incorrect because some continental plates (for example, the Indian Plate) are smaller than oceanic plates (for example, Pacific Plate).

D   is incorrect because some continental plates (for example, North American Plate) are larger than oceanic plates (for example, the Juan de Fuca Plate).

4.   A

A   is correct because the plates separate from each other at a divergent boundary.

B   is incorrect because the plates slide past each other at a transform boundary.

C   is incorrect because the plates collide at a convergent boundary.

D   is incorrect because at a divergent boundary, the plates move apart. A plate is sometimes subducted under another plate at convergent boundaries.

5.   B

A   is incorrect because there is no indication on this map that the Scotia Plate and the Pacific plate are converging.

B   is correct because there is a convergent boundary between the Cocos Plate and the Caribbean Plate.

C   is incorrect because there is no indication on this map that the South American Plate and the African plate are converging.

D   is incorrect because the North America Plate and the Antarctic Plate do not share a boundary.

Lesson 3 Quiz

1.   C   3.   A   5.   B
2.   D   4.   D

1.   C

A   is incorrect because tension causes faulting, not folding.

B   is incorrect because shear stress leads to faulting, not folding.

C   is correct because when rocks are compressed, they fold as a result.

D   is incorrect because the term "normal" applies to a type of fault that is the result of stress.

2.   D

A   is incorrect because the blocks in a strike-slip fault move in different directions.

B   is incorrect because the blocks in a strike-slip fault move primarily horizontally.

C   is incorrect because the blocks in a strike-slip fault move primarily horizontally.

D   is correct because the blocks in a strike-slip fault move horizontally in opposite directions.

3.   A

A   is correct because in a syncline, the rocks in the center of the fold, are the youngest; in an anticline, the rocks in the center of the fold are the oldest.

B   is incorrect because in a syncline, the rocks in the center of the fold are the youngest; in an anticline, the rocks in the center of the fold are the oldest.

C   is incorrect because a monocline does not have a center.

D   is incorrect because in an anticline, the rocks in the center of the fold are the oldest; also, a monocline does not have a center.

4.   D

A   is incorrect because tension is the stress that pulls the two walls apart, and L labels a wall, not a stress.

B   is incorrect because the footwall is the wall that remains higher when the hanging wall moves down, and *L* labels the wall that moves down.

C is incorrect because the fault line divides the footwall from the hanging wall, and *L* labels a wall, not a line.

D is correct because the hanging wall is the wall that drops down, as shown at *L* in the figure.

5. B

A is incorrect because rocks are made up of minerals both before and after deformation.

B is correct because the deformation of rocks changes the shape and size of rocks. Deformation is the result of tectonic plate movement that causes compression, tension, or shear stress on rocks.

C is incorrect because during deformation, rocks remain the same kind of rock.

D is incorrect because deformation does not change the composition of rocks.

Lesson 4 Quiz

1. D   3. B   5. B
2. B   4. C

1. D

A is incorrect because shield volcanoes have gentle slopes.

B is incorrect because composite volcanoes have both quiet and violent eruptions, so their slopes are not as steep as those of cinder cone volcanoes.

C is incorrect because pyroclastic is not a type of volcano.

D is correct because cinder cone volcanoes have violent eruptions that form steep sides.

2. B

A is incorrect the lava is molten rock that has reached Earth's surface while magma is molten rock found beneath Earth's surface.

B is correct because lava is defined as magma that has reached Earth's surface.

C is incorrect because ash, cinders, and blocks are types of solid material that come out of a volcano.

D is incorrect because all molten rock beneath Earth's surface is called magma.

3. B

A is incorrect because hot spots are not found along rift zones.

B is correct because hot spots form over mantle plumes.

C is incorrect because hot spots are not found along divergent boundaries.

D is incorrect because hot spots are not found along convergent boundaries.

4. C

A is incorrect because both lava and pyroclastic materials erupt onto Earth's surface.

B is incorrect because shield volcanoes have quiet eruptions with lava flows.

C is correct because pyroclastic materials are ejected from violent eruptions.

D is incorrect because lava is associated with nonviolent eruptions.

5. B

A is incorrect because point 1 is pointing to lava, a type of molten material expelled from a volcano's vent.

B is correct because molten material, ash, and dust are ejected from a volcano's vent.

C is incorrect because magma is molten material found within a volcano.

D is incorrect because an ash cloud is made up of materials that has already been expelled from a volcano's vent.

Lesson 5 Quiz

1. D   3. D   5. A
2. B   4. A

1. D

A is incorrect because the epicenter is not necessarily the place that has the greatest damage, but it is the place directly above the focus.

B is incorrect because earthquakes always take place at a fault where rock has been deformed.

C is incorrect because an earthquake has only one epicenter, which is located directly above the focus.

D is correct because the epicenter is a point directly above the focus, which may be on a part of the fault line that is not directly below a point where the fault reaches the surface.

2. B

A is incorrect because the rock in the interior of a plate is not stronger than the rock at the boundary.

B is correct because the source of energy for earthquakes comes from deformation of rocks by tectonic plate motion, which generally happens at plate boundaries.

C is incorrect because earthquakes are caused by the energy of moving plates, not the energy transferred from magma.

D is incorrect because earthquakes happen at all types of plate boundaries, not just boundaries where one plate moves over another.

3. D

A is incorrect because tension takes place when plates diverge, not when they converge.

B is incorrect because stretching takes place when plates diverge or move past one another, not when they converge.

C is incorrect because shear stress takes place at transform plate boundaries.

D is correct because compression takes place when two plates push together.

4. A

A is correct because the greatest amount of energy released on

Earth's surface is at the epicenter of the earthquake.

B is incorrect because the greatest amount of energy released on Earth's surface is at the epicenter of the earthquake.

C is incorrect because the energy travels from the epicenter in all directions.

D is incorrect because energy decreases as distance from the epicenter increases.

5. A

A is correct because tsunamis are generally caused by undersea earthquakes.

B is incorrect because tsunamis caused by meteorites are rare, and no meteorite strike took place then.

C is incorrect because wind cannot generate a tsunami.

D is incorrect because earthquakes, not typhoons, cause tsunamis.

Lesson 6 Quiz

1. D   3. A   5. D
2. C   4. A

1. D

A is incorrect because earthquakes begin below Earth's surface where there is sudden movement along a fault.

B is incorrect because the epicenter is directly above, not directly below, an earthquake's focus.

C is incorrect because an earthquake's focus is the position below Earth's

surface where an earthquake begins.

D is correct because *epicenter* is defined as the point on the surface directly above an earthquake's focus.

2. C

A is incorrect because the amount of time between the arrival of the P wave and the arrival of the S wave would increase.

B is incorrect because even though the waves would take longer to reach the seismograph, the amount of time between the arrival of the P wave and the arrival of the S wave would increase.

C is correct because the lag time between the arrival of the P wave and the arrival of the S wave increases with distance from the epicenter.

D is incorrect because the lag time between the arrival of the P wave and the arrival of the S wave increases with distance from the epicenter, not decreases.

3. A

A is correct because earthquake intensity diminishes with travel distance.

B is incorrect because earthquake intensity diminishes with travel distance.

C is incorrect because earthquake intensity diminishes with travel distance.

D is incorrect because earthquake intensity

diminishes with travel distance.

4. A

A   is correct because the amount of displacement along a fault is one measure of moment magnitude.

B   is incorrect because the distance from the focus determines an earthquake's intensity at a given location, not its magnitude.

C   is incorrect because damage is a measure of the intensity of an earthquake, not magnitude.

D   is incorrect because the distance from the epicenter determines an earthquake's intensity at a given location, not its magnitude.

5. D

A   is incorrect because circular or rolling describes the motion of one type of surface wave.

B   is incorrect because side-to-side describes one aspect of the motion caused by S waves.

C   is incorrect because up-and-down describes one aspect of the motion caused by S waves.

D   is correct because P waves cause the alternating expansion and contraction of rock particles in the direction of travel.

Lesson 1 Alternative Assessment

Take Your Pick: Earth's Physical and Compositional Layers

Picturing Earth's Layers: Posters show Earth's solid compositional layers. The layers are labeled and briefly described.

What Are Your Thoughts?: Cards describe what student knew about Earth's compositional layers before completing the lesson and the most interesting thing student learned about Earth's compositional layers during the lesson.

Down to the Core: Venn diagrams correctly identify the similarities and differences between Earth's inner and outer cores.

The Layer Quiz: Cards show the names of Earth's layers and some of the properties of the layers.

Seeing Inside: Presentations describe how seismic waves and their speed help scientists learn about the inside of Earth.

Your Turn to Teach: Lesson accurately describes the layers of the solid Earth.

Blast from the Past: Timelines show past theories about Earth's internal structure in the correct sequence.

What's in a Layer?: Presentations compare and contrast the two ways of looking at Earth's internal structure.

Lesson 2 Alternative Assessment

A Puzzling Picture: Puzzle pieces fit together to form one large landmass. Student demonstrations and explanations accurately portray plate tectonics.

Plate Interview: Interview presents ten questions and answers. The answers are ones that could have come from Alfred Wegener in 1912.

Sea-floor Spreading: Writing describes the process of sea-floor spreading and uses the Mid-Atlantic Ridge as an example. Description tells how material reaches the surface and why the ridge is higher than the surrounding oceanic plates.

Density Differences: Poem or song explains how density differences below Earth's plates cause the plates to move and change shape.

Flipbook: Flipbook shows what happens at a convergent boundary, a divergent boundary, and a transform boundary.

Collision Diorama: Diorama includes labels, and shows convergent boundaries formed between two continental plates, a continental plate and an oceanic plate, or two oceanic plates.

Lesson 3 Alternative Assessment

Quiz Cards: Three cards include the terms *compression*, *tension*, and *shear stress*. Three other cards include the definitions for these terms.

To a Fault: Poster describes and illustrates the three types of faults.

Flipping Forward: Flipbook shows how a folded mountain forms.

On the Range: Description describes a famous mountain

range, what type of range it is, and the way it formed.

Plate Talk: Skit describes what might happen to a tectonic plate that is pushing against another plate, what might happen to the other tectonic plate, and why.

You're the Expert!: Report notes where the oldest rock is located in the fold, describes the shape of the fold, and how the syncline occurred.

Lesson 4 Alternative Assessment

Earthquake Poster: Poster shows how an earthquake occurs and how elastic deformation can take place. Labels show the focus, epicenter, and fault.

Word Swap: Puzzles use one vocabulary word from the lesson, and include a paragraph that tells about the word.

Earthquake Events: Flipchart shows the sequence of events that cause an earthquake and how the ground moves during an earthquake.

Earthquake Article: Article describes being in an earthquake, what caused the quake, when it hit, what the aftermath was like, and how people's lives were affected.

Shaky Story: Story tells what happens during an earthquake, what the characters do, and how they react.

Boundary Action: Models show a divergent boundary, a convergent boundary, and a transform plate boundary. The direction of movement is labeled.

Lesson 5 Alternative Assessment

Vocabulary: The root of volcano is listed, along with other words in the lesson that contain the root. Each word is defined.

Illustrations: Trading cards show and label the three types of volcanoes, and describe how each type is similar to and different from the other types.

Analysis: Presentations describe how Earth's surface might be different if volcanoes did not exist and which landforms and landmasses might not exist if it weren't for volcanoes.

Details: Letters explain that volcanoes can also form in other areas, describe the other areas, and explain how these volcanoes occur.

Models: Models accurately depict a shield volcano. They also label the volcano's vent, lava flow, and magma chamber. Models describe how a shield volcano is different from and similar to other types of volcanoes.

Lesson 6 Alternative Assessment

Newspaper Article: Articles will include a concise but complete summary of earthquakes. Articles will include relevant statistics on the local, fictional earthquake and be written with an appropriate news reporting style using proper grammar.

Triangulation Map: Maps will reflect strong research skills. Written summaries will clearly define an epicenter and describe how one is located using triangulation.

Seismogram: Seismogram selection should reflect strong research skills. Written summaries will clearly define a seismogram and accurately describe how lag times can be used to determine the magnitude of earthquakes.

Earthquake Locations: Written explanations will clearly describe the factors that cause earthquakes to occur more frequently in certain locations. Students will include information on fault lines and plate tectonics in their descriptions.

Before and After: Collages will use pictures that depict an obvious before and after difference in a location or locations that experienced an earthquake. Students should cite any sources they have used.

Lasting Construction: Written explanations should include details about construction materials, methods, and designs that can withstand earthquakes. Explanations should also make a clear connection between earthquake-prone areas and using the described construction materials.

Performance-Based Assessment

See Unit 4, Lesson 4

1. Answers will vary. Sample answer: The thick mixture will flow more slowly.

2. Answers will vary. Sample answer: More gas can escape from a thin mixture.

10. The thin mixture had more bubbles. The thick mixture had fewer bubbles.

11. Thinner mixtures allow more gas to escape than thick ones do.

12. The mixture with 5 mL cornstarch spread out more. This mixture flowed more quickly because it was thin and runny. The mixture with 15 mL cornstarch spread out very little because it was thick and stiff.

13. A high-silica lava would be stiffer and would flow more slowly. A low-silica lava would be thinner and would flow more quickly.

14. Thick, stiff lava that is high in silica would be more likely to plug a volcano.

15. The magma is probably low in silica.

Unit Review

Vocabulary

1. **mantle See Unit 4, Lesson 1**

2. **Plate tectonics See Unit 4, Lesson 2**

3. **Folding See Unit 4, Lesson 3**

4. **volcano See Unit 4, Lesson 4**

5. **earthquake See Unit 4, Lesson 5**

Key Concepts

6. C	10. B	14. B
7. C	11. C	15. B
8. A	12. C	16. C
9. B	13. C	17. D

6. C See Unit 4, Lesson 4

A is incorrect because magma is below Earth's surface and lava is above Earth's surface.

B is incorrect because lava is not solid material.

C is correct because magma is below Earth's surface and lava is above Earth's surface.

D is incorrect because magma is lava once it erupts and lava erupts both in the ocean and on land.

7. C See Unit 4, Lesson 2

A is incorrect because some continental plates are not necessarily larger than oceanic plates. Larger is not synonymous with thicker.

B is incorrect because some continental plates are not necessarily smaller than oceanic plates.

C is correct because continental crust is thicker than oceanic crust.

D is incorrect because oceanic crust is thinner than continental crust.

8. A See Unit 4, Lesson 5

A is correct because the focus is the point at which an earthquake originates, which is beneath the surface of Earth and usually along a fault.

B is incorrect because it is the earthquake epicenter, which is the area on Earth's surface that is directly above the focus.

C is incorrect because it is the fault along which the earthquake occurred, not the focus.

D is incorrect because the series of circles labeled D represent wavefronts of energy traveling away from the focus, but not the focus itself.

9. B See Unit 4, Lesson 4

A is incorrect because a calm eruption usually does not involve pyroclastic materials.

B is correct because a violent eruption typically releases pyroclastic materials.

C is incorrect because a fast eruption doesn't necessarily mean pyroclastic materials will be released.

D is incorrect because a slow eruption is probably calm, but also doesn't necessarily mean pyroclastic materials will be released.

10. B See Unit 4, Lesson 2

A is incorrect because plates move horizontally past one another along Earth's surface at a transform boundary.

B is correct because plates move away from each other at divergent boundaries and commonly form rift valleys and mid-ocean ridges.

C is incorrect because plates do not come together at a divergent boundary.

D is incorrect because plates do not collide or cause subduction at a divergent boundary.

11. C See Unit 4, Lesson 5

A is incorrect because a fault boundary traces a fault, which cannot be shown by one dot.

B is incorrect because the focus is the point beneath Earth's surface where an earthquake originates.

C is correct because the epicenter is the point on Earth's surface directly above the focus.

D is incorrect because a tectonic plate boundary is between two plates and cannot be shown by one dot.

12. C See Unit 4, Lesson 2

A is incorrect because the inner core is solid and the outer core is liquid.

B is correct because the inner core is solid and the outer core is liquid.

C is incorrect because the inner core is not in the form of a gas.

D is incorrect because the outer core is not in the form of a gas.

13. C See Unit 4, Lesson 4

A is incorrect because condensation occurs when a gas changes into a liquid.

B is incorrect because conduction is the transfer of energy from one object to another by direct contact.

C is correct because convection is the transfer of energy by the movement of matter.

D is incorrect because radiation is the transfer of energy by electromagnetic waves.

14. B See Unit 4, Lesson 1

A is incorrect because A is the core, B is the mantle and C is the crust.

B is correct because A is the core, B is the mantle, and C is the crust.

C is incorrect because A is the inner and outer core, B is the mantle, and C is the crust.

D is incorrect because although A is the core, B is not the crust—it is the mantle, and C is not the mantle—it is the crust.

15. B See Unit 4, Lesson 1

A is incorrect because these five layers are divided based on physical properties, not composition.

B is correct because these five layers are divided based on physical properties.

C is incorrect because these five layers are divided based on physical properties, not chemical properties.

D is incorrect because these five layers are divided based on physical properties, not on elemental properties.

16. C See Unit 4, Lesson 3

A is incorrect because the line marked *J* does not represent a river.

B is incorrect because the lines marked by *J*s are not pointing consistently to a single rock layer.

C is correct because the lines marked by *J*s are pointing to a fault line.

D is incorrect because the focus is not a point on the line.

17. D See Unit 4, Lesson 5

A is incorrect because faults exist in rocks throughout the world, including rocks in Africa.

B is incorrect because the size of a continent does not determine whether or not earthquakes occur.

C is incorrect because Africa is within a single tectonic plate, so there are no plate boundaries within the continent.

D is correct because the focus is not a point on the line.

Critical Thinking
18. See Unit 4, Lesson 2

- At a convergent boundary, the tectonic plates move toward each other. Mountain building, volcanism, subduction, and large earthquakes occur at these boundaries.

- At a transform boundary, the two plates slide past each other. Mountain building and volcanism are uncommon along the boundaries. Earthquakes can occur often along these boundaries.

- Earthquakes occur along both types.

19. See Unit 4, Lesson 1

- A is the lithosphere, B is the asthenosphere, and C is the mesosphere.

- The lithosphere is the crust and rigid upper mantle, and is divided up as tectonic plates, which "float" on top of the asthenosphere. The asthenosphere is slow-flowing rock and the mesosphere is the lower part of the mantle, and the rock flows even more slowly here. Convection in the mantle is a driving force of the tectonic plates of the lithosphere.

20. See Unit 4, Lesson 6

- The Moment Magnitude scale measures earthquake strength based on the size of the area of the fault that moves, the average distance that the fault moves, and the rigidity of the rocks in the fault. The larger the number is, the stronger the earthquake was.

- The Richter scale measures the ground motion from an earthquake to find the earthquake's strength.

- Measurements from the Richter scale could be misleading because each time the magnitude increases by one unit, the measured ground motion is 10 times greater. Therefore, a magnitude 2 has 10 times the ground motion as a magnitude 1, and magnitude 3 has 100 times the ground motion as a magnitude 1! You can see how this exponentially increases as you go up the scale.

Connect Essential Questions

21. See Unit 4, Lesson 3 and Lesson 4

- The movement of tectonic plates produces stress that causes rock to deform (strain). Strain can result in folds and/or faults (this depends on many factors not covered). Faults can create fault block mountains after a very long time of uplift and erosion. Large folds can create folded mountains. When two plates come together at a convergent margin, subduction can cause volcanic activity, resulting in volcanic mountains.

- Fault block mountains can also form when tension from divergent boundaries causes faults and the blocks of rock on either side of the fault move up or drop down relative to other block.

- Sometimes volcanic activity beneath Earth's surface forces magma upward towards Earth's surface. The forces associated with upwelling can cause uplift of the crust, and the lava and other material (such as ash and cinder) erupted from the vent can build up into a mountain over time.

Unit Test A
Key Concepts

1. C	6. D	11. C
2. C	7. D	12. B
3. C	8. B	13. D
4. D	9. A	14. C
5. A	10. C	15. B

1. C

A   is incorrect because oceanic crust is denser than continental crust.

B   is incorrect because oceanic crust is both thinner and denser than continental crust.

C   is correct because oceanic crust is made up of denser materials, and is also much thinner than continental crust.

D   is incorrect because oceanic crust is thinner than continental crust.

2. C

A   is incorrect because both magma and lava are molten rock.

B   is incorrect because lava is magma, or molten rock, that has reached Earth's surface.

C   is correct because magma chambers can be deep underground. Lava is magma that has reached Earth's surface.

D   is incorrect because a volcano is any place where gas, ash, or melted rock come out of the ground.

3. C

A   is incorrect because more earthquakes occurred along the tectonic plate boundaries than occurred within the ocean basins.

B   is incorrect because more earthquakes occurred along the tectonic plate boundaries than occurred within the continental landmasses.

C   is correct because most of the earthquakes are concentrated along the edge of the Pacific plate.

D   is incorrect because more earthquakes occurred along the edge of the Pacific Ocean than occurred along the edge of the Atlantic Ocean.

4. D

A   is incorrect because lava is not a type of volcano.

B   is incorrect because shield volcanoes are made of quiet lava flows.

C   is incorrect because, although composite volcanoes have violent eruptions, they also have quiet eruptions that produce gentle lava flows.

D is correct because cinder cone volcanoes have violent eruptions that produce pyroclastic materials.

5. A

A is correct because the anticline and syncline folds in the mountains are clearly visible.

B is incorrect because erosion is a process that wears down mountains, the evidence for which are not clear in the figure.

C is incorrect because a volcanic mountain would have different features, including magma chambers, and fissures.

D is incorrect because fault-block mountains form when stress causes blocks of rock to move up or down, relative to other blocks of rock.

6. D

A is incorrect because, although magnetic reversals are recorded in the rocks at divergent boundaries, the process of magnetic reversals occurs deep within Earth's core.

B is incorrect because crustal materials are recycled into the mantle at convergent boundaries, not divergent boundaries.

C is incorrect because divergent boundaries only produce oceanic crust.

D is correct because mid-ocean ridges form at divergent boundaries on the ocean floor where two oceanic plates are pulling away from each other.

7. D

A is incorrect because the footwall moves up when a normal fault occurs.

B is incorrect because the hanging wall drops down when a normal fault occurs.

C is incorrect because, when a normal fault occurs, most of the movement is up and down, not side to side.

D is correct because the hanging wall drops down when a normal fault occurs.

8. B

A is incorrect because tall buildings will sway more than short buildings during an earthquake.

B is correct because short buildings will sway less during an earthquake; also, steel and wood are able to flex and absorb some of the earthquake's energy.

C is incorrect because tall buildings will sway more than short buildings during an earthquake, and because brick and concrete are less flexible than steel or wood.

D is incorrect because brick and concrete are less flexible than steel or wood.

9. A

A is correct because a crater is the relatively small, steep-walled depression around a volcano's vent caused by eruptions.

B is incorrect because a fissure is an opening in Earth's surface.

C is incorrect because a caldera is a large depression that can form after a volcanic eruption when the magma chamber empties. The vent no longer exists.

D is incorrect because although a lava plateau is a steep-walled feature, it does not form around a vent.

10. C

A is incorrect because surface waves can travel in any direction along Earth's surface.

B is incorrect because body waves can travel in any direction.

C is correct because body waves travel outward from an earthquake's focus, and surface waves are confined to Earth's surface.

D is incorrect because surface waves travel outward from the epicenter, not the focus, and because body waves travel below Earth's surface.

11. B

A is incorrect because letter A represents the lithosphere.

B is correct because letter B represents the asthenosphere.

C is incorrect because letter C represents the mesosphere.

D is incorrect because letter D represents the outer core.

12. B

A is incorrect because earthquakes take place beneath the surface.

B is correct because an earthquake happens when

elastic rebound causes a sudden release of energy.

C   is incorrect because earthquakes are not caused by formation of holes beneath the surface.

D   is incorrect because currents in the oceans and atmosphere have no effect on the stress that causes earthquakes.

13. D

A   is incorrect because plate tectonics is a theory that describes the movement of the plates on the asthenosphere, which is the soft layer of the mantle.

B   is incorrect because chemical composition, not structural features, is used to identify these layers of Earth.

C   is incorrect because Earth is divided into five layers based on physical properties.

D   is correct because the three layers of core, mantle, and crust are identified based on the chemical substances they contain.

14. C

A   is incorrect because folded mountains form as a result of compression, not tension.

B   is incorrect because the collision of continents causes compression, not tension.

C   is correct because the collision of continents causes compression, which forms folded mountains.

D   is incorrect because fault-block mountains form as a result of tension, not compression.

15. B

A   is incorrect because the ocean existed before the plates collided.

B   is correct because magma from the mantle rises to Earth's surface and erupts as lava from volcanoes.

C   is incorrect because the figure does not show a divergent boundary between two oceanic plates.

D   is incorrect because the figure shows a convergent boundary.

Critical Thinking
16.

• a description of either one plate sliding under another or of two continental plates colliding

• an explanation that the rock deforms and then returns to its undeformed shape, releasing energy (e.g., *As the two plates push into one another, rocks are deformed. When the rocks return to their shape through elastic rebound, energy is released, causing waves in the crust*; etc.)

Extended Response
17.

• description of outer core as liquid

• description of inner core as solid

• explanation that liquid outer core means less frictional drag (e.g., *The inner core can rotate faster because of the fact that the outer core is liquid. This means that the inner core can move more freely than if the outer core was solid*; etc.)

Unit Test B
Key Concepts

1. A	6. B	11. B
2. B	7. B	12. B
3. B	8. B	13. A
4. B	9. B	14. B
5. B	10. A	15. C

1.   A

A   is correct because oceanic crust has much higher proportions of iron and magnesium than continental crust has, which makes it denser and heavier.

B   is incorrect because the higher proportions of iron and magnesium in the oceanic crust makes it denser and heavier.

C   is incorrect because silicon and aluminum are major constituents of both oceanic and continental crust; oceanic crust does not have higher proportions of these elements than continental crust does.

D   is incorrect because silicon and aluminum are major constituents of both oceanic and continental crust; oceanic crust does not have higher proportions of these elements than continental crust does.

2.   B

A   is incorrect because magma is not solid rock; it is molten rock.

B   is correct because magma is molten rock.

C   is incorrect because volcanic ash is made up of very tiny particles of solid rock.

D   is incorrect because cones are small mountains that result from eruptions of magma; they are not molten rock.

3. B

A   is incorrect because hurricanes and typhoons do not lead to earthquakes.

B   is correct because earthquakes generally take place along plate boundaries.

C   is incorrect because tsunamis are just one result of earthquakes, not a cause.

D   is incorrect because earthquakes result from stresses between tectonic plates, not from the weight of water above them.

4. B

A   is incorrect because lava is not a type of volcano.

B   is correct because shield volcanoes have quiet eruptions that are not usually associated with pyroclastic flows.

C   is incorrect because composite volcanoes can have violent eruptions associated with pyroclastic flows.

D   is incorrect because cinder cone volcanoes have violent eruptions associated with pyroclastic flows.

5. B

A   is incorrect because in a syncline, the youngest rock layers (those farthest away from Earth's interior) are in the center of the fold, and the rock limbs slope up from the center to form a trough.

B   is correct because in anticlines, the oldest rock layers (those closest to

Earth's interior) are in the center of the fold, and the rock limbs slope down from the center to form an arch.

C   is incorrect because the structure labeled *K* is an anticline, which contains both old and young rock layers.

D   is incorrect because the structure labeled *K* is an anticline, which contains both old and young rock layers.

6. B

A   is incorrect because crustal materials are recycled into the mantle at convergent boundaries, not divergent boundaries.

B   is correct because as two plates pull away from each other at a divergent boundary, mantle material rises upward to form new crust between the diverging plates.

C   is incorrect because plates move away from each other rather than sliding past each other at divergent boundaries.

D   is incorrect because at a divergent boundary, the plates move apart, not together.

7. B

A   is incorrect because the footwall does not move up along a reverse fault.

B   is correct because the hanging wall moves up along a reverse fault due to compressional tension.

C   is incorrect because the hanging wall moves up along a reverse fault.

D   is incorrect because the walls mainly move up or down, not from side to side, along a reverse fault.

8. B

A   is incorrect because solid bedrock lessens the effects of surface waves.

B   is correct because sediments with water can intensify the effects of surface waves; also, more energy is transmitted to the surface by shallower earthquakes.

C   is incorrect because less energy is transmitted to locations that are farther from an earthquake's epicenter.

D   is incorrect because earthquakes that originate at greater depths are less able to transmit energy to the surface than those at shallower depths.

9. B

A   is incorrect because a crater is a depression with steep walls around a volcano's vent.

B   is correct because a fissure is a crack or an opening in Earth's surface.

C   is incorrect because a caldera is a large depression formed when the roof of the magma chamber collapses.

D   is incorrect because a lava plateau is a landform created by layers of hardened lava.

10. A

A   is correct because P waves and S waves are both types of body waves and because they both travel faster than surface waves.

B   is incorrect because P waves and S waves are both types of body waves, not surface waves.

C   is incorrect because surface waves are a type of body wave, not surface wave.

D   is incorrect because P waves are body waves, not surface waves.

11. B

A   is incorrect because letter B represents the asthenosphere, the soft layer of the mantle on which the tectonic plates move.

B   is correct because letter C represents the mesosphere.

C   is incorrect because letter D represents the outer core, the hot liquid surrounding the inner core.

D   is incorrect because letter E represents the inner core, the hot center made mostly of iron and nickel.

12. B

A   is incorrect because tsunamis are one result of earthquakes.

B   is correct because earthquakes are caused by movement of tectonic plates along a fault. Tectonic plates can move past each other, collide, or overrun each other.

C   is incorrect because earthquakes happen when the potential energy from rock movement, not in a fault, is suddenly released.

D   is incorrect because shaking of the lithosphere is a result of an earthquake.

13. A

A   is correct because the core is at the center of Earth.

B   is incorrect because the mantle is the middle layer of Earth, located between Earth's crust and core.

C   is incorrect because the lithosphere is the solid, outer layer of Earth that consists of the crust and the rigid upper part of the mantle.

D   is incorrect because the asthenosphere is part of the mantle.

14. B

A   is incorrect because folded mountains form as a result of compression, not tension.

B   is correct because the separation of continents causes tension, which forms fault-block mountains.

C   is incorrect because the separation of continents causes tension, which forms fault-block mountains.

D   is incorrect because fault-block mountains form as a result of tension, not compression.

15. C

A   is incorrect because the figure shows a convergent boundary and not a transform boundary.

B   is incorrect because the figure shows a convergent boundary and not a divergent boundary.

C   is correct because a mountain range can form when two tectonic plates converge.

D   is incorrect because the figure shows a convergent boundary and also because continents do not buckle and form mountain ranges at divergent boundaries.

Critical Thinking
16.

• a description of two plates sliding horizontally past one another

• an explanation that the rock deforms and then returns to its undeformed shape, releasing energy (e.g., *As the two plates move past one another, rocks are deformed. When the rocks return to their shape through elastic rebound, energy is released, causing waves in the crust*; etc.)

Extended Response
17.

• description of outer core as liquid

• description of inner core as solid

• description of a design or a model that will illustrate this difference (e.g., *To model the outer core, I would fill a bowl with water to show half of the outer core. To model the inner core, I would float a ball in the middle of the bowl. This would demonstrate how the solid inner core [ball] is surrounded by the liquid outer core [water]*; etc.)

End-of-Module Test

1. A	11. A	21. C
2. B	12. B	22. A
3. C	13. B	23. B
4. C	14. D	24. D
5. C	15. B	25. B
6. C	16. D	26. D
7. D	17. A	27. A
8. D	18. B	28. C
9. C	19. D	29. A
10. D	20. A	30. A

1. A See Unit 4, Lesson 6

A   is correct because P waves and S waves are both types of body waves.

B   is incorrect because the term *Richter* refers to an earthquake magnitude scale, not a type of seismic wave.

C   is incorrect because the term *Richter* refers to an earthquake magnitude scale, not a type of seismic wave.

D   is incorrect because surface waves are not a type of body wave.

2. B See Unit 1, Lesson 4

A   is incorrect because loess is formed when wind deposits layers of fine-grained sediment and the deposits build up, not when layers of rock are deposited on one another.

B   is correct because loess is formed when wind deposits layers of fine-grained sediment and the deposits build up.

C   is incorrect because loess is formed when wind deposits layers of fine-grained sediment and the deposits build up, not when layers of sediment are deposited by moving rivers.

D   is incorrect because loess is formed when wind deposits layers of fine-grained sediment and the deposits build up, not when layers of ice are deposited by snow and turn into ice.

3. C See Unit 1, Lesson 2

A   is incorrect because the water that seeps into the soil will cause chemical weathering.

B   is incorrect because erosion is not a type of chemical weathering.

C   is correct because the rocks that are moved to the surface will be exposed to more physical weathering agents than underground rocks.

D   is incorrect because exfoliation is not the process by which the tortoise breaks up rocks.

4. C See Unit 3, Lesson 2

A   is incorrect because sedimentary rock can also change into metamorphic rock under intense heat and pressure.

B   is incorrect because intense heat and pressure can also change igneous rock into metamorphic rock.

C   is correct because both igneous rock and sedimentary rock can change into metamorphic rock under conditions of intense heat and pressure.

D   is incorrect because both igneous rock and sedimentary rock can change into metamorphic rock during the rock cycle.

5. C See Unit 3, Lesson 1

A   is incorrect because these materials contain nonmetallic elements.

B   is incorrect because none of these materials are made up of only one type of atom.

C   is correct because all of these materials contain a combination of silicon and oxygen atoms.

D   is incorrect because all of these materials contain a combination of silicon and oxygen atoms. Therefore, they are silicate minerals.

6. C See Unit 4, Lesson 2

A   is incorrect because the two plates are not moving apart, as they would at a divergent boundary.

B   is incorrect because the two plates are not sliding past each other horizontally along Earth's surface, as they would at a transform boundary.

C   is correct because the two plates are colliding or moving toward each other as shown by the arrows.

D   is incorrect because the two plates are in motion as shown by the arrows.

7. D See Unit 2, Lesson 2

A   is incorrect because igneous rocks may form large crystals as they cool, but sedimentary rocks are made from deposited sediment.

B   is incorrect because sedimentary rock is deposited one layer on top of another, making horizontal layers.

C   is incorrect because sediment is usually deposited in layers, and the metamorphic process may create swirling bands when metamorphic rocks are formed.

D is correct because sediment is deposited one layer on top of another, thus making horizontal layers in sedimentary rocks.

8. D See Unit 1, Lesson 5

A is incorrect because this choice does not include all of the primary factors that affect soil formation, and it also includes three that do not—rainfall, temperature, and wind.

B is incorrect because this choice is missing some of the primary factors that affect soil formation—parent rock and some types of living things, such as bacteria.

C is incorrect because this choice does not include all of the primary factors that affect soil formation, and it also includes one that does not—sunshine.

D is correct because these factors work together to form soil.

9. C See Unit 1, Lesson 2

A is incorrect because ice can push rocks apart, but minerals cannot dissolve in ice.

B is incorrect because wind causes abrasion and is an agent of physical weathering.

C is correct because the minerals in certain rocks can be oxidized by oxygen in air.

D is incorrect because gravity is an agent of physical weathering.

10. D See Unit 2, Lesson 3

A is incorrect because 25% left means that two half-lives

have taken place, so the sample would be 2.6 billion years old.

B is incorrect because 25% left means that two half-lives have taken place, so the sample would be 2.6 billion years old.

C is incorrect because 25% left means that two half-lives have taken place, so the sample would be 2.6 billion years old.

D is correct because 25% left means that two half-lives have taken place, so with a half-life of 1.3, 2 x 1.3 = 2.6, so the sample would be 2.6 billion years old.

11. A See Unit 4, Lesson 5

A is correct because rock becomes deformed between earthquakes as tectonic plates move.

B is incorrect because energy in rock decreases during an earthquake, not between earthquakes.

C is incorrect because faults do not open and close.

D is incorrect because the energy in rock increases as plates move.

12. B See Unit 1, Lesson 3

A is incorrect because a delta is a fan-shaped mass of material deposited at the mouth of a stream.

B is correct because the place where land and a body of water meet is the definition of a shoreline.

C is incorrect because groundwater is the water that is beneath Earth's surface.

D is incorrect because an alluvial fan is a fan-shaped mass of material deposited by a stream when the slope of the land decreases sharply.

13. B See Unit 1, Lesson 1

A is incorrect because living and once-living things are part of the biosphere.

B is correct because the atmosphere is a mixture of nitrogen, oxygen, and other gases that surrounds Earth.

C is incorrect because the mixture of nickel and iron below the mantle describes the core.

D is incorrect because liquid water is the hydrosphere.

14. D See Unit 2, Lesson 2

A is incorrect because if area 2 is overturned, rock X will appear in rock layer 2. Rock X is also found in rock layer 1 in area 1. Therefore, rock layer 1 in area 1 is the same age as the inverted rock layer 4 in area 2.

B is incorrect because area 1 is undisturbed, so the youngest layer is the top layer.

C is incorrect because the older layers are the top layers in area 2, which has been overturned.

D is correct because the rock layers in area 2 have been overturned, so the youngest layer is the bottom layer in this case. Therefore, rock layer 5 is the youngest rock layer in area

2, and it is younger than rock layer 1 in area 1.

15. B See Unit 4, Lesson 2

A is incorrect because a continental rise is a gently sloping section of the continental margin.

B is correct because continental drift is the hypothesis that all the continents were once part of one supercontinent that broke apart.

C is incorrect because a continental shelf is a gently sloping section of the continental margin.

D is incorrect because a continental slope is a steeply inclined section of the continental margin.

16. D See Unit 2, Lesson 1

A is incorrect because a sinkhole is a depression in the ground.

B is incorrect because a sedimentary rock might not contain any trace of an organism that once lived.

C is incorrect because crystals are solids whose particles are arranged in a definite pattern.

D is correct because a fossil is the physical evidence of an organism that once lived.

17. A See Unit 4, Lesson 4

A is correct because lava flows onto Earth's surface during nonexplosive volcanic eruptions. This also happens during explosive volcanic eruptions.

B is incorrect because magma does not flow onto Earth's surface.

C is incorrect because composite is a type of volcano, not a type of volcanic material.

D is incorrect because pyroclastic materials are ejected during explosive eruptions.

18. B See Unit 1, Lesson 4

A is incorrect because the retreat of a continental glacier does not form valleys.

B is correct because alpine glaciers can turn V-shaped valleys into U-shaped valleys like the one shown by causing erosion and breaking up rock.

C is incorrect because the kettle lakes are not part of the valley shown in the illustration.

D is incorrect because the deposition of glacial drift would not form a valley.

19. D See Unit 4, Lesson 1

A is incorrect because the core is the innermost layer of Earth.

B is incorrect because a plate is a part of Earth's lithosphere.

C is incorrect because the crust is the outermost layer of Earth.

D is correct because the mantle is the hot, convecting layer of rock between the crust and the core.

20. A See Unit 3, Lesson 3

A is correct because when magma erupts from a volcano, it is called lava.

B is incorrect because magma is hot, liquid rock by definition.

C is incorrect because lava forms extrusive igneous rocks and magma forms both extrusive and intrusive igneous rocks.

D is incorrect because foliated and nonfoliated rocks are two different types of metamorphic rocks, not igneous rocks.

21. C See Unit 1, Lesson 5

A is incorrect because of 100 g, 25 percent is air and silt is 18 percent for only 43 percent of the 100 g sample.

B is incorrect because silt is 18% and sand is 18% for only 36% of the 100 g sample.

C is correct because air is 25% and water is 25% for only 50% of the 100 g sample.

D is incorrect because clay is 9% and organic matter is 5% for only 14% of the 100 g sample.

22. A See Unit 3, Lesson 3

A is correct because the approximate age of Earth is 4.6 billion years.

B is incorrect because Earth is approximately 4.6 billion years old, not 4.6 million years old.

C is incorrect because Earth is approximately 4.6 billion years old, not 46,000 years old.

D is incorrect because Earth is approximately 4.6 billion years old, not 4,600 years old.

23. B See Unit 2, Lesson 4

A is incorrect because Pangaea had already split into separate continents before the Cenozoic Era began.

B is correct because in the late Paleozoic era, the continents converged to form Pangaea.

C is incorrect because Pangaea had already split into separate continents before the Triassic Period began.

D is incorrect because Pangaea had already split into separate continents before the Jurassic Period began.

24. D See Unit 4, Lesson 5

A is incorrect because faults exist in rocks throughout the world.

B is incorrect because Africa is a single tectonic plate, so there are no plate boundaries within the continent.

C is incorrect because the fact that there were no earthquakes has to do with the locations of tectonic plate boundaries, not with landmass.

D is correct because the continent of Africa is located on a single continental tectonic plate; so, there are no plate boundaries along which earthquakes would take place.

25. B See Unit 4, Lesson 1

A is incorrect because the rigid upper part, not the fluid part, of the mantle is also part of the lithosphere.

B is correct because the rigid upper part of the mantle is also part of the lithosphere.

C is incorrect because the rigid upper part, not the soft moving part, of the mantle is also part of the lithosphere.

D is incorrect because the rigid upper part of the mantle is

part of the lithosphere, and the lower part of the mantle is slow flowing, not stationary.

26. D See Unit 4, Lesson 3

A is incorrect because a syncline is characteristic of a folded mountain, which is formed by compression, not tension.

B is incorrect because an anticline is characteristic of a folded mountain, which is formed by compression, not tension.

C is incorrect because a folded mountain is formed by compression, not tension.

D is correct because tension is stress that stretches and pulls a body apart. This process can create fault-block mountains.

27. A See Unit 1, Lesson 3

A is correct because a sinkhole forms when the roof of a cave collapses.

B is incorrect because a sinkhole forms when the roof of a cave collapses; sinkholes do not form from canyons.

C is incorrect because a sinkhole forms when the roof of a cave collapses; sinkholes do not form from ponds.

D is incorrect because a sinkhole forms when the roof of a cave collapses; sinkholes do not form from valleys.

28. C See Unit 4, Lesson 4

A is incorrect because radiation is the transfer of energy by electromagnetic waves.

B is incorrect because conduction is the transfer of

energy from one object to another by direct contact.

C is correct because convection is the transfer of energy by the movement of matter.

D is incorrect because condensation occurs when a gas changes into a liquid.

29. A See Unit 1, Lesson 1

A is correct because saltwater accounts for about 97% of Earth's water, leaving 3% that is fresh water.

B is incorrect because fresh water accounts for only 3% of Earth's water.

C is incorrect because fresh water accounts for only 3% of Earth's water.

D is incorrect because the oceans contain about 97% of Earth's water, and water in the oceans is salty.

30. A See Unit 3, Lesson 2

A is correct because flowing water can break down rock, cause rock fragments to scrape against each other and against the sand on the stream bottom, and result in pebbles that are worn smooth.

B is incorrect because the force of gravity would not cause the rounding of pebbles in a stream.

C is incorrect because the movement of ice would imply that the pebbles were rounded by a glacier.

D is incorrect because freezing and thawing would not cause the rounding of pebbles in a stream.

Visual Answers

Unit 1, Unit Test B, Item 13

- a drawing of a valley with a
  U-shaped profile

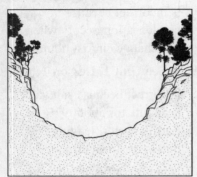